Praise for *Gratitude: A Way of Teaching*

"This book is an excellent tool for educators and parents to transform the students' disposition from victim to advocate. It addresses how to model behavior in order to combat the denial of accountability, treat the cancer of complaining, and reverse the effects of emotional atrophy. Each chapter provides activities ('Let's talk about it') to instill skills in our students to become a valuable contributor in our society. *Gratitude: A Way of Teaching* is about future-proofing by investing in our future one gratitude at a time."—**Dr. Greg A. Doss**, Bartow County School System CTAE Coordinator

"In a time of tests, accountability, and burnout, *Gratitude: A Way of Teaching* beautifully encourages teachers and students to connect to their own and each other's humanity by stopping for a moment and asking, 'What is wonderful about life?'"—**Vicki Zakrzewski**, Ph.D., Education Director, Greater Good Science Center at UC Berkeley

"In *Gratitude: A Way of Teaching,* Mr. Griffith does a superb job at giving teachers practical strategies for making their students grateful. Following these strategies, and with patience and persistence, we *can* significantly influence the children in our own personal worlds. And, if we do, that will influence programs, clubs, schools, and other institutions in the community, too. Our society needs this book more than ever. With teachers like Mr. Griffith in the classroom waving the 'gratitude flag,' we parents have yet another reason to be grateful."—**Jeffrey J. Froh**, Psy.D., associate professor of psychology, Hofstra University; co-author of *Making Grateful Kids: The Science of Building Character*

"Gratitude is a difference-maker. With the power to heal, energize, and change lives, we need gratitude in the classroom more than ever. Weaving together real world examples, inspirational stories, and the latest science, Owen M. Griffith explains why. *Gratitude: A Way of Teaching* should be required reading for teachers, administrators, parents, and anyone else who has a stake in our children's future. You will be challenged, edified, and stirred to take a fresh look at this timeless virtue and see why we owe our children the gift of gratitude."—**Robert A. Emmons**, Editor-in-Chief, *The Journal of Positive Psychology*; author of *Gratitude Works!* and *Thanks! How the New Science of Gratitude Can Make You Happier*

"Exciting new research has shown that gratitude may play a vital role in our schools. In *Gratitude: A Way of Teaching*, Owen M. Griffith writes about how he has used this research in his classroom. I believe that this book will help many people. In a very practical way, Griffith shows how gratitude can be incorporated into the schools. Filled with inspiring examples and many practical suggestions, this book can be used to improve the gratitude of students in your classroom, and perhaps more importantly, it should help teachers generate a more grateful attitude toward their students. My hope is that this book will provide the spark to develop new ways to incorporate gratitude into the school setting."—**Dr. Philip Watkins**, Professor of Psychology, Eastern Washington University

"This is an important book that inspires us to revitalize our classrooms through the lenses of gratitude, calling for teachers, parents, and students to create a joyful and kind environment so that we all may thrive."—**Erik Herndon**, classroom teacher at Centennial Academy, Atlanta, GA

Gratitude

Gratitude

A Way of Teaching

Owen M. Griffith

With Gratitude,
Owen Griffith

ROWMAN & LITTLEFIELD
Lanham • Boulder • New York • London

Published by Rowman & Littlefield
A wholly owned subsidiary of The Rowman & Littlefield Publishing Group, Inc.
4501 Forbes Boulevard, Suite 200, Lanham, Maryland 20706
www.rowman.com

Unit A, Whitacre Mews, 26-34 Stannary Street, London SE11 4AB

British Library Cataloguing in Publication Information Available

Library of Congress Cataloging-in-Publication Data Available

Library of Congress Cataloging-in-Publication Data

ISBN 978-1-4758-2062-1 (cloth : alk. paper) ISBN 978-1-4758-2063-8 (pbk. : alk. paper) — ISBN 978-1-4758-2064-5 (electronic)

∞™ The paper used in this publication meets the minimum requirements of American National Standard for Information Sciences—Permanence of Paper for Printed Library Materials, ANSI/NISO Z39.48-1992.

Printed in the United States of America

Author's Note

The names of the students in this book have been changed for their protection.

This book is dedicated to my wife, Tricia, and son, Asher, with deep gratitude and appreciation for their growing, unconditional love and for inspiring this book.

Also, this book is dedicated to all the teachers out there: the teachers who taught me, inspired me, and now are in the trenches (classrooms) with me. We are all teachers in some way; may we all teach with gratitude.

Contents

Foreword

Matthew, a twelve-year-old middle school student who lives within a wealthy suburb, had a home life quite different than that of his peers: he and his mother had found themselves in a long-term shelter because of a financial crisis, and Matthew had to commute to school by public bus rather than the German imports his friends' parents used to drop off their children.

As winter approached, Matthew continued to come to school dressed in jeans and T-shirts with just a thin sweatshirt for covering, prompting one teacher, Mrs. Riebe, to give him a wool sport jacket from the donation bin at her church. It was a kind gesture, but a sixth grader wearing a sport jacket in a prosperous public school means one thing: a bully target. Matthew, however, wasn't bullied, nor was he embarrassed about wearing an oversized jacket. Instead, he smiled from ear to ear. "Check out this cool jacket Mrs. Riebe gave me; I love it. I can't stop thanking her," he'd say to his friends and other teachers. His infectious positivity was so appealing, even other kids recognized and respected it.

The circumstances in which Matthew lived might make many children feel envious, cheated, angry, and resentful. Yet Matthew felt incredibly grateful to his teachers and friends because his mother, despite the constraints on her time and finances, had instilled a sense of gratitude in Matthew; this had a profound effect on his approach to life.

My colleagues and I collected nearly two thousand essays on what gratitude means to teens, and Matthew's essay was among them. He wrote, "My life wouldn't be the same without the people who've helped me succeed. I'm thankful to God and my family, friends, and even my teachers for helping me improve my life."

This story of an adolescent who lives below the material standards of most of his peers and has to make much more of an effort to get to school and participate in extracurricular activities is a small but profound example of the power that gratitude can have on a young person's emotional well-being, relationships, spirituality, and success. In fact, my experience working with at-risk children and adolescents supports this assumption. But Matthew is no ordinary kid because he has learned to harness a virtue that's been long-revered, but historically underappreciated: gratitude.

I met Matthew while working as a school psychologist. Seeing him walk down the hall and smile from ear to ear while wearing a wool sport jacket intended for a much older gentleman is burned in my memory forever. It was a defining moment for me. How did Matthew become so grateful? Why isn't he envious of the other kids wearing designer labels? Does he even realize that his new jacket is totally uncool? My quest for understanding gratitude development in youth began in that hallway.

After reviewing the psychological literature on gratitude in kids, I found noticeable holes that needed filling. One such hole was the lack of research on gratitude in the early stages of life. Until 2005, there were no studies that I knew of examining gratitude and well-being in children. Then, in 2006, psychology professors and researchers Nansook Park and Christopher Peterson conducted a content analysis of parents' descriptions of children's strengths, gratitude being one. They found that out of the twenty-four strengths examined, gratitude had the strongest relation to life satisfaction. Witnessing gratitude's power in the children and adolescents I worked with and counseled, coupled with this latest finding, I decided to commit myself to a research program looking to understand the measurement, development, and enhancement of gratitude in youth.

Perhaps the most commonly used technique for boosting gratitude—one that Mr. Griffith used with his fourth-grade class—is a gratitude journal. For my first study on gratitude in youth, I asked middle school students simply to list five things for which there were grateful daily for two weeks, and I compared these students to others who were writing about hassles in their life or basic daily life events. Keeping a gratitude journal was related to more optimism and life satisfaction and to fewer physical complaints and negative emotions.

Most significantly, compared to the other students, students who kept a gratitude journal reported more satisfaction with their school experience (i.e., find school interesting, feel good at school, think they are learning a lot, and are eager to go to school) immediately after the two-week period, a result that held up even three weeks later. Expressions of school satisfaction included: "I am thankful for school," "I am thankful for my education," and "I am thankful that my school has a track team and that I got accepted into honor society."

School satisfaction is positively related to academic and social success (and Mr. Griffith does a great job in this book describing the cutting edge research supporting this relation). Many early and late adolescents, however, indicate significant amounts of dissatisfaction with their school experience. Therefore, inducing gratitude in students via keeping a gratitude journal may be a viable intervention for mitigating negative views of school and academics while promoting positive views about school and academics. Holding such a positive view predisposes students to improving both their academic and social competence and may help motivate them to get the most out of school.

Another exercise we've tested, one that you will read about in *Gratitude: A Way of Teaching*, is the gratitude visit. Here, students write a letter to someone who had helped them but whom they'd never properly thanked; the students read their letter to him or her in person, then later discuss their experience with others who also completed a gratitude visit. To illustrate, one seventeen-year-old girl wrote and read the following letter to her mother:

I would like to take this time to thank you for all that you do on a daily basis and have been doing my whole life. . . . I am so thankful that I get to drive in with you [to school] every day and . . . for all the work you do for our church. . . . I thank you for being there whenever I need you. I thank you that when the world is against me that you stand up for me and you are my voice when I can't speak for myself. I thank you for caring about my life and wanting to be involved . . . for the words of encouragement and hugs of love that get me through every storm. I thank you for sitting through countless games in the cold and rain and still having the energy to make dinner and all the things you do. I thank you for raising me in a Christian home where I have learned who God was and how to serve him. . . . I am so blessed to have you as my mommy and I have no idea what I would have done without you.

Findings from this indicated that students who began the study low in positive emotions reported more gratitude and positive emotions immediately after the study, and greater positive emotions two months later, compared with students who didn't do a gratitude visit.

Building on this research, and research by colleagues, we have identified several key principles that adults can use to promote gratitude in children and adolescents—principles that we have incorporated into our own gratitude curriculum. This curriculum is intended to subtly instill grateful thinking in youth without requiring an explicit focus on gratitude. It emphasizes three key principles that can support a gratitude journal, a gratitude visit, or simply the practice of gratefulness in everyday life. They are:

- **Notice intentions:** Try to encourage youth to appreciate the thought behind gifts they receive—to consider how someone noticed their need and acted on it. Research suggests this goes a long way toward cultivating "an attitude of gratitude" among children and adults alike. For kids in particular, knowing that others believe in them and their potential motivates self-improvement. To get children and adolescents to reflect on the intentions behind the gifts they receive, adults can prompt them with a question such as, "Can you think of a time when a friend (or parent, teacher, or coach) noticed something you needed (e.g., lunch) or remembered something you care about (e.g., collecting feathers) and then provided you with those things?" As kids give examples, adults could have them elaborate: "How did you know they helped you on purpose?" "How did you feel after they helped you?"
- **Appreciate costs:** We also find it important to emphasize that when someone is helpful, that person usually sacrifices time or effort to provide the help. For example, adults could ask, "What are some things your friend gave up to help you with that project?" or say, "Wow, for your friend to come play tag with you, he had to stop playing soccer, which I know is his favorite game." An adult could also point out "how nice it was for that child to let you use the computer instead."
- **Recognize the value of benefits:** Adults can also foster gratitude by reminding youth that when others help us, they are providing us with "gifts." This is one reason why, in our gratitude curriculum, we prompt children to focus on the personal value of the kind acts of others. One way adults can bring this up is to have kids complete the sentence stem "My day (or life) is better because . . ." and give examples such as "my teacher helped me when I didn't understand something" or "my coach showed me how to be a better basketball player."

Studies of our gratitude curriculum have found that children's ability to think gratefully can be strengthened, and with this change comes improvements in their moods. A weekly version of the curriculum produced these effects up to five months later. A daily version had immediate effects (two days later) and led children to write 80 percent more thank you cards to their parent-teacher association; even their teachers found them happier.

In *Gratitude: A Way of Teaching*, Mr. Griffith does a superb job of giving teachers practical strategies for how students can see the value of gratitude in their lives. Following these strategies, and with patience and persistence, we *can* significantly influence the children in our own personal worlds, and, if we do, that *will* influence programs, clubs, schools, and other institutions in the community too. So I ask you to accept my challenge, and dedicate yourself to helping a child become more grateful. Our society needs this more than ever. Now's the time. And with teachers like Mr. Griffith in the classroom waving the "gratitude flag," we parents have yet another reason to be grateful.

—Jeffrey J. Froh, Associate Professor,
Hofstra University, and co-author of
Making Grateful Kids: The Science of Building Character

Preface

If there was something that you knew could help people, a powerful tool that was free, would you want to share it? Most people would answer with a strong, "Yes, of course!" Well, that is what gratitude is to me. Gratitude may be looked at as a tool, something we can learn to implement to improve our lives and classrooms. But it is also so much more than that. Gratitude is a way of living and teaching. Daily, we can choose to practice gratitude and experience the numerous positive benefits for us and all those around us.

As I reflect on utilizing gratitude for more than ten years in my classroom, I see how practicing gratitude has empowered me to teach more effectively, appreciate my individual students, grow in my profession, and enjoy life. I am able to model one of the most important lessons in life, having a positive attitude, especially about the aspects of life that challenge me. In fact, three years ago, I was voted teacher of the year at my school, a direct result of practicing conscious gratitude in my life, in my classroom, with my colleagues, and in my personal life.

Personally, I started utilizing gratitude in my life before I became a teacher and when I was able to integrate gratitude into my classroom, I saw a transformation, a paradigm shift, where I was enabled to become a better teacher, approaching my job with more joy and energy. Just as important, the students were changing in front of my eyes, growing emotionally and socially, as well as intellectually and academically.

In 2006, I introduced gratitude in my classroom with a simple gratitude list to start our day. At that point, not much scientific research existed to support this practice, but with the practical evidence materializing in front of me, I was encouraged and kept using it, finding new avenues and new applications for gratitude. The students powered and encouraged our effort with gratitude, finding new ways to apply it in their lives, showing me that gratitude is much more than a pleasant emotion, but an action and a way of living.

Now, almost ten years later, the scientific research is in, and it has confirmed that practicing gratitude in our lives and classrooms helps on many levels. Using the tools of gratitude improves the lives of adults and students in many powerful and transformative ways. This book is about gratitude being a way of teaching and a way of living. Even if you are not a teacher, you will find things to help in your life. And if you are a parent, you may find some of these tools especially useful. I am grateful for the opportunity to share my experience with you.

Here is a quote that encapsulates some of these ideas about using gratitude to see all the miracles in our lives:

> People usually consider walking on water or in thin air a miracle. But I think the real miracle is not to walk on water or in thin air, but to walk on earth. Every day we are engaged in a miracle which we do not even recognize: a blue sky, green leaves, the black curious eyes of a child–our own two eyes. All is a miracle.

Thich Nhat Hanh,
global spiritual leader, poet, and peace activist

Introduction

One looks back with appreciation to the brilliant teachers, but with gratitude to those who touched our human feelings. The curriculum is so much necessary raw material, but warmth is the vital element for the growing plant and for the soul of the child.

–Carl Jung

WHY GRATITUDE?

Since the beginning of time, teachers have been naturally integrating gratitude into education. I don't claim to have invented the idea of applying gratitude in the classroom. In this book, I will share my experience and success with utilizing gratitude in my classroom and my life. I will also explore the wealth of research conducted in the area of gratitude and education.

Gratitude is a numbers game. The more often we practice it and find new ways to express it in our lives and classrooms, the more it becomes habit and a deep and vital aspect of our lives. Gratitude is like a million dollar grant that we get one dollar at a time. It is not always instant gratification, although every time we practice it, we can feel better and more positive. Gratitude helps recalibrate our brains in a positive way, allowing us to see all the good going on in our classrooms and the world.

Today, we live in a "microwave" culture with so much at our fingertips that transforming our lives or classrooms is also thought of as something to be done instantaneously. Many books have been written about self-improvement and also about teaching, offering quick fixes and magic bullets to change everything at once.

However, gratitude is more than a fad diet or get-rich-quick scheme that sounds promising and gives hope until instant success is not achieved and we return to our original outlook. Gratitude is so much more than a quick fix; it is like a tool to use in our lives and in our classrooms, rewiring our brains and reshaping our lives.

Even though gratitude is not some panacea that will solve all problems instantaneously, it is a powerful device that may propel us to make changes that will become permanent in our lives and classrooms, affecting everything we do. By applying scientific research and practical activities, gratitude may become a conscious choice through which we filter life, and we may start making more positive choices in our responses to our students, families, and society. When I really started using gratitude daily, everything changed, but the biggest change was in me.

GRATITUDE CAN CHANGE YOUR CLASSROOM AND YOUR LIFE

Teaching is a challenging endeavor. With all the demands on a teacher's time and energy, it is easy to lose the enthusiasm that brought us into the classroom. In addition, teachers have recently had new requirements added to their load, including standardized testing and dealing with changing curriculums.

However, there is good news. Recent research and personal experience have shown that gratitude, a simple yet powerful tool, may be applied in our classrooms to improve the culture as well as raising the student's grades and goals.

I have not always been a grateful person. I did not have a gloomy disposition, but I did have a somewhat cynical nature that seemed to rob the joy from my life. Even now, gratitude does not always come easy for me. Some days, I do not feel grateful and can fall into a negative groove. But this is when I see the efficacy of gratitude as I simply write a quick gratitude list and feel a little better about everything.

Incrementally, gratitude has become easier for me as I practice it daily and really try to flex my gratitude muscles. Practicing gratitude is like working out physically. Sometimes I don't want to work out, but when I do, I am always rewarded. I see the world and everyone in it in a much more positive light. If I can be consistent and make gratitude part of my routine, I see how beautiful life is again.

I started using gratitude fifteen years ago when I worked in an office for a food company. Working in the logistics and customer service department, my shift went from 7 AM to 5 PM daily. Toward the end of just about every day, I would feel tired and start to think negatively about everything.

After work, I found myself bringing that pessimism to my home life. A friend, who always seemed to be smiling and in a good mood, told me that her secret to happiness and resilience in life was to keep a "Gratitude Journal," where she wrote at least five things that she was grateful for every day. My friend added a challenge by telling me that no repeats were allowed on the list.

Initially, as I started my gratitude journal, it felt awkward and I wondered if it was a waste of time. However, after the first week, I felt a subtle, yet powerful, change occurring. Being extremely busy, I found I actually had to make a reminder pop up on my computer screen at 4 PM every day or I would forget to do the gratitude journal.

Even if the day was hectic, I would stop what I was doing and write the gratitude list. I found it only took a couple minutes and always refreshed and refocused my energy. That negativity that used to snowball all day began to dissipate with the implementation of the gratitude log. After establishing this new habit, every night, by the time I got home, I was able to greet my wife with a smile and enjoy our evenings together.

As I kept using this simple gratitude activity, some of the subtle incremental changes became more pronounced. I found myself reflecting on the good things that happened to me. What surprised me even more, when life was challenging, I would find something positive inside any negative situation. For example, when I had to stay late and work some overtime, I was immediately resentful. But when I took a breath and wrote a quick gratitude list, I became grateful that I had a job and that I would receive some overtime pay on my next paycheck.

Most people I know who have tried making a daily gratitude list of at least five things to be grateful for and stuck with it for at least two weeks with a willing attitude have experienced tremendous rewards. You may make the list on paper, create a word document, or use your smartphone. There are apps that make this easy. For me, a written list is more powerful than a mental list.

However, for those that found the gratitude journal didn't work for them, we were able to find other gratitude activities that fit their personality better, like verbally or visually expressing gratitude. Then, they were also able to enjoy the benefits of gratitude. So, don't give up if one activity doesn't work.

ED

When I told my good friend Ed that I was writing this book, he asked if I would use his story of gratitude. It is powerful story, showing how gratitude may be applied in any situation.

---

*Ed travels for his work. In the middle of the summer's oppressive heat in Loui-
siana, he got a flat tire. He didn't have a spare, so he used his cell phone to call
for help. It was over one hundred degrees outside and the humidity added an
uncomfortable stickiness to an already miserable day. Going back into his truck,
he found his air conditioning also wouldn't work.*

*He then called me, telling me his truck had broken down, it was sweltering,
the air conditioning didn't work, he was late for his appointment, his shirt was
soaked with sweat, and the man had just arrived with a new tire for his truck.*

*I responded, "Why don't you do a gratitude list? Start with that guy who is
fixing your flat." He said, "Thanks a lot," sat back in his seat, sweating, thinking that was a wasted phone call. How could someone be grateful when their
car broke down, they are late to a business meeting, and it is over one hundred
degrees?*

*Surprisingly, he later told me that he did make a quick mental gratitude list, and
he said it worked. He realized that these things were really minor inconveniences.
Slowly, it dawned on him that he had a car and many people didn't. He had a
good job, when others were struggling with unemployment, and he had help from
the gentleman fixing his problem. After the tire was fixed, he dried his shirt and
made it to the next appointment with a smile. Gratitude salvaged the day.*

Sometimes, gratitude will work in the most unlikely circumstances if we
just try it. Since that experience, Ed still uses gratitude in his life and now
he reminds me to be grateful when I forget. And some days, I do need that
friendly reminder.

Grateful for Everything, Even Problems

One coworker said he did not realize how negative some people were until
he started to practice gratitude. I have another friend who puts his gratitude
list on his refrigerator, so he sees it every time he goes to get something to
eat. When I was hanging out with him and went to his refrigerator, it made
me feel wonderful when I saw that I was on his gratitude list. My brother,
who teaches high school, just started using a gratitude list with his students
and called me the other day, raving about the excitement it has generated in
his classroom.

While working customer service and logistics, my job was to find solutions when things went wrong. I knew gratitude was working for me when I
could be grateful for the "problems" at work. Some days, I would even see
that these challenges allowed me to find new solutions and implement new
protocols to avoid the same problematic situations again. In the past, I would

have just complained about these situations and felt drained after dealing with them.

GRATITUDE AT WORK

One afternoon, years ago, when I worked in logistics, the act of writing this gratitude list brought about a humorous incident. As the gentle reminder came up on my computer screen to "Do your Gratitude List," I took a few moments from my busy day to make my daily addition to the list. Astonishingly, when I took this action, I always felt better and re-energized enough to get through the rest of the workday.

On that day, I finished the list, saved it, and was about to get back to work when I heard a voice over my shoulder say, "That does not look work related." Turning around in my cubicle, I saw my boss looking over my shoulder at my gratitude list. Thus far, I had not shared the joys of gratitude with my boss.

In a nanosecond, I had to decide how to respond to my boss—should I be honest or make up some cover story? I am happy to report that I went with the honest answer, "You are right. This isn't directly work related. But, it is a gratitude list. It helps me focus on what is good in life and this actually helps me stay positive. I can even help our customers and my co-workers more if I practice gratitude." Okay, I guess I did get a little carried away in my reply, but I did believe that gratitude was changing the way I related to customers and my co-workers.

Coming back to the situation, I studied the face of my boss intently to see his reaction. His stoic countenance did not give anything away. He waited another second and said, "That gratitude list is working. We have noticed how positive you are and it is affecting everyone else around here. Keep up the good work, and by the way, we just thought you were so positive because you were on drugs." That last part just made us both laugh.

Incidentally, the next year at that job, as I kept practicing gratitude in my life and at work, I was awarded "Employee of the Year" out of 250 workers. I attribute that to practicing gratitude and making the conscious choice daily to find gratitude in every situation at work. That was challenging at times, and I didn't always do it. Sometimes, I just made it through the day, but I still did my gratitude journal. Interestingly, making my gratitude list when gratitude was hard to find felt the most powerful.

At that point in my life, many factors came together, and I thought about changing careers to become an educator. In my job, I was training others and a colleague told me that I would be a great teacher. My parents had given me the gift of education, and I wanted to give that gift back to others. I made the monumental decision to switch careers and become a teacher. The day I left that job, the chief executive officer of the company came out with a cake that said, "I wish I could be in Mr. Griffith's class."

AN EAGER NEW TEACHER:
THE DREAM AND THE REALITY

My first year teaching, I entered the classroom with idealistic dreams. I went through extra training in pedagogy that tempered those lofty goals and gave me many tools I was anxious to use. I taught seventh-grade science in an inner-city school and saw 120 students a day. Sadly, within a few weeks, dealing with a multitude of challenges, I quickly slipped into survival mode and questioned my decision to become a teacher. But, small and sometimes tremendous miracles did happen that kept me moving forward.

Because I had been practicing gratitude and keeping a gratitude list for a few years, I still kept a decent attitude through all the challenges of that first year. A fellow teacher commented that even though my first year was tough and she saw me struggle, I kept the most positive attitude she had ever seen. That positive outlook did help me, but I didn't see how it could apply with the students yet.

THE CHALLENGES AND THE
MIRACLES OF THE FIRST YEAR

Of all the things I have done in my life, getting through my first year of teaching was by far my most challenging undertaking. During that first year, I am thankful that I would occasionally reach those transcendent moments where I did connect with the student and felt the magic that happens when the classroom unites in learning.

Angel

During my first week of teaching, one day I came across one of my students, Angel, sitting in the hallway with some sheet music. I asked, "Are you a musician?" She said, "No, but I love to sing and I am learning a new song." I asked her if she would sing for me, but Angel said, "No, Mr. Griffith, I am too shy." As I walked away I said, "Someday, when you are ready, you will sing for me."

Then, a month later, Angel saw me in the hallway and said, "Mr. Griffith, I am ready today." I tried to think about what she meant. Through the tornado of activity that first month, I forgot about that previous interaction. But she brought out the sheet music, and I suddenly remembered it all. I realized that she had been working for a month on the song and getting her courage up just for this day. I asked her if she would perform for the class, but she said, "No, I will sing just for you."

That day, when the students all exited the classroom, she closed her eyes, and a voice came out of her that fit her name. It truly seemed like an angel had entered the classroom as she sang. I closed my eyes and enjoyed listening to her share her musical talent.

As I listened, I also realized the power to inspire we have as teachers and that when we challenge our students, they will often respond positively. In addition, she inspired me to bring my guitar into the classroom and share music with my students, integrating it into the lessons I would teach. While she grew in her courage through this interaction, I grew in my ability to connect with my students by seeing that there are many ways to reach students outside the traditional paradigms.

As the year progressed, I kept doing the things that worked, but classroom management was getting in the way of my lessons. This was a tough school, and I was breaking up fights in my classroom, as well as dealing with students who had given up on life by the seventh grade. I wanted to reach all these students so much, but I could only connect with a small fraction of them.

Many nights, I would wake up at 3 AM, haunted by all the things going wrong with my teaching. This is when I would do a personal gratitude list and still find the good things happening among all the apparent problems. This kept me going through those darkest hours. Just when I thought of quitting and going back to my old career, a major miracle happened.

Robert

Robert was a tough seventh grader who didn't seem to care about school or anything else. By his own admission, he was on the brink of joining a gang and failing every subject. When I would pass out the science assignment for the day, he would say, "Mr. G., science doesn't mean anything in my life." Then, he would ceremoniously crumple up the assignment and throw it in the trash saying, "I'll take an 'F' for the day." This bothered me tremendously, and I tried different things to reach him, but nothing seemed to get through.

Then, one day after winter break, I handed out a new assignment about the scientific method. Surprisingly, Robert looked intently at the page and said, "Will you help me with this Mr. G?" After what he said registered in my brain, I quickly went to his desk and guided him through the scientific method. On the way home that night, I found myself smiling and wondering what happened to Robert. The next thing that ran through my mind was, "Will this change last, or was it a one-day anomaly?"

The next day, we delved further into the scientific method and Robert asked more questions. Even more shocking, he started helping some of his fellow students who used to throw the papers away right along with Robert.

Robert's turnaround came at my darkest hour in the classroom. I don't know if I would have kept going if it hadn't been for this minor miracle. But I realized it wasn't just a minor miracle. When a student who was thinking about joining a gang and failing every subject turned around and not only got an A in my science class, but also got straight As in every subject by the end of the year, helped other students in academics, and stayed out of trouble, I realized I was a small part of a major miracle.

When I had one award to give at the end of the year, I gave it to Robert and felt overwhelmed with joy as he walked across the stage at the assembly to receive his award. His parents came to the ceremony and were beaming with the same joy we all shared that day.

Astonished and encouraged by this student's turnaround, I asked my mentor if she had a student like this every year and she said that she has not had any students like this in her seven years of teaching. I examined Robert's dramatic about-face with his other teachers, but we could not locate a specific reason that changed him and got him on a positive track.

When I asked Robert what had happened, he said, "You never gave up on me and kept trying with me Mr. G." I was reminded of a saying from a pedagogy professor who would gently remind us, *"All it takes to change a student's life is the appropriate adult at the appropriate time."*

Even with this phenomenal student, by the end of my first year, I was exhausted and wanted to take a year off to re-examine my decision to become a teacher. I almost became part of that sad statistic that says almost half the teachers leave the profession in the first five years. But, a great opportunity was presented to teach fourth graders at a new school in a new city. This time, I had some experience and knew that I would do things differently.

GRATITUDE—THE MISSING ELEMENT IN THE CLASSROOM

To start the new year of teaching, I knew I needed to get a better classroom management program. I was paired with another teacher who had eleven years of experience and was a master teacher. As we planned for the year, she noted that I had a tremendously positive attitude and asked how I cultivated this sunny disposition. I told her that I work at it by keeping a gratitude journal. Intrigued and a bit skeptical, she said she wanted to try it.

Within a few weeks, she commented on how much it helped her. One day as we were planning for the first day of school, I had the inspiration of trying gratitude in the classroom. I realized that this could be a breakthrough. If it worked for me and others, it would work for the students. Also, this was a chance to interject some of my personality into my teaching and dramatically improve the culture of the classroom.

So, when the students arrived, we started a gratitude journal from the first day of class. That was over ten years ago, and as those original students enter college now, many of them still keep their gratitude logs, though some have updated them to their computers or smartphones.

Grateful Parent

Recently, a parent shared with me that she was cleaning up her son's room and found something underneath his bed. Surprised, she opened the book and saw it was his gratitude journal that he had started in my class and was still updating into high school. Carefully, she returned it to his hiding place with a smile, knowing her son had taken the practice of gratitude to heart. She said she was glad her son would be practicing gratitude throughout his life, that it was an "essential" skill that would benefit him in every endeavor he encounters in life.

Gratitude was one of the missing elements for me in the classroom, bringing about a positive and optimistic culture that only seemed to improve as the year went on. Furthermore, gratitude had a cascading effect that gave me more energy to devote to every aspect of teaching, from planning lessons to dealing with conflict between students, to keeping the students interested in school as the year dragged on.

Cecilia

A few years ago, one of my students, Cecilia, looked at me in the middle of a math lesson with concern and said, "Mr. Griffith, can we all do a gratitude list together?" My heart rose, and I was so proud of her. After we concluded the activity, I profusely thanked her and told her that she had truly made gratitude part of her life.

I asked her what prompted the request to do a gratitude list. She simply said, "I wanted to do a gratitude list with you because you look so stressed out today." That made me smile, but it also showed how people around us can gently remind us to be grateful and brighten our rough days.

CONCLUSION

This book gives educators solution-based methods and resources to promote a positive classroom culture, as well as enables schools to elevate students' engagement and academic achievement. In addition, activities are provided that will help teachers improve their own lives as well as their students' lives. Success stories and step-by-step instructions are also included in order to implement gratitude in classrooms and schools.

Grounded in scientific research, this book will delve into numerous integral aspects of gratitude as it relates to education, including:

- Applying gratitude activities in many forms and enjoying the benefits they bring
- Exploring positive psychology, the foundation of gratitude
- Challenging the culture of complaining and replacing it with gratitude
- Combatting materialism and entitlement with gratitude and altruism
- Understanding the barriers to implementing gratitude and dispelling them
- Healing losses in life with gratitude for students and educators
- Guidelines for using technology and interjecting gratitude into our students' lives
- Balancing our busy lives with mindfulness in conjunction with gratitude
- Helping teenagers utilize gratitude successfully and overcoming their resistance
- Encouraging the families of our students to embrace gratitude and a variety of activities to help it become a permanent part of their lives
- Integrating activities and exploring resources to help educators stay energized with gratitude throughout the school year

Writing this book has been a pleasure and the entire process has helped me grow with gratitude. As you read this book, feel free to contact me with questions as well as to share your challenges and successes with gratitude. You will join the growing community of educators who are finding gratitude to be an important and effective tool in the classroom. My contact information is in the appendix.

Part I

OVERVIEW OF GRATITUDE

Chapter One

The Roots of Gratitude

Positive Psychology

When it comes to life the critical thing is whether you take things for granted or take them with gratitude.

—G.K. Chesterton

RESEARCH-BASED POSITIVE PSYCHOLOGY

One of the most promising developments in the area of psychology over the past twenty years is the robust area of research in positive psychology, particularly in the area of gratitude. Ten years ago, when implementing gratitude in the classroom, only a limited amount of research existed about applying gratitude in an educational setting. Due to the hard work of many social scientists, we now have a body of research, grounded in science, that supports implementation of gratitude activities and other tools in our lives and in our classrooms as a way to improve classroom culture and increase student achievement.

FROM LEARNED HELPLESSNESS TO LEARNED OPTIMISM

To begin with, let's look at the research from a pioneering researcher, Dr. Martin E. P. Seligman, a leader in the field of positive psychology. Interestingly, almost fifty years ago, he pioneered research on "learned helplessness," which helped explain why some people "give up" in certain situations. Now, Seligman has a pioneered researcher in an area of psychology that deals with the polar opposite, "learned optimism."

An informative book by Dr. Seligman, *Flourish,* gives us insight into this positive shift in psychology and some simple yet powerful tools which we can implement in our lives and classrooms. In this book, Seligman states that the study of psychology used to be dominated by focusing on the negative and the dysfunctional. Psychology used the "disease" model, attempting to find what was wrong with people.

However, more recent research has been concentrating on the positive areas of psychology in the following areas:

- Gratitude
- Optimism
- Forgiveness
- Compassion
- Happiness
- Altruism

Furthermore, Seligman says that we often spend too much time thinking about what goes wrong and not enough time about what is going right in our lives. There is an evolutionary basis for this. If our ancestors spent all their time celebrating the good things and not preparing for adversity, they may not have been able to survive one of the many crisis or catastrophes that came along, like the Ice Age.

Naturally, in our lives, thinking about things that go wrong and solving problems is helpful. However, focusing too much on the negative aspects in life can lead to depression and anxiety. This is where positive psychology exhibits its ability to help us change from negative rumination to positively savoring the good aspects of life. The question becomes, "How do we overcome our brains' built-in bias toward negativity?"

Seligman and his colleagues began rigorously experimenting with interventions and activities that may be practiced to increase people's fulfillment and contentment with life. Quickly, gratitude stood out as a research area with effective interventions and long-lasting results.

Traditionally, the study of gratitude was kept in the fields of theology or philosophy as only a "virtue." However, in numerous studies of positive psychology, gratitude exhibited an effective means to provide strength and resilience in times of adversity or emotional upheaval. Furthermore, practicing gratitude helped produce many positive benefits psychologically and physically.

THE WHAT WENT WELL EXERCISE

On the positive side, research-based activities have been shown to help "reprogram" our brains for a more positive outlook. Seligman conducted a powerful study called "The What Went Well Exercise," also known as "Three Blessings." In this intervention, people were asked to set aside ten minutes at night before they went to sleep to write down three things that went well that day and why they went well. A journal, computer, or even a smartphone may be used for this. It is important to physically record this instead of just making a mental list because it helps imprint it deeper in the mind.

The three good things recorded do not need to be monumental; it could be as ordinary as, "My son got an A on a quiz at school," or "I had a satisfying cup of coffee with a friend." However, participants were encouraged also to write about the more substantial events, like, "I got a promotion at work," or "my sister had a healthy baby."

After each event has been recorded, people were asked to answer the following question, "Why did this happen?" For instance, if someone wrote "My son got an A on a quiz at school," this could be expanded to: "My son got an A on a quiz at school because he had time and resources to study and grow academically."

Delving deeper into "why" an event happened may seem awkward or even forced at first, but Seligman encourages perseverance with this exercise for at least a week as we remind ourselves that we are "re-programming" our negative bias. Like any challenge, when we keep trying, it gets easier and may even become an enjoyable exercise. Seligman asserts that this practice will raise our feeling of well-being and help alleviate any depression we may be experiencing. Later in this book, we will look at how powerful this exercise is when utilized with students.

THE GRATITUDE VISIT

Another potent application of positive psychology in our lives is the "Gratitude Visit." In this exercise, Seligman asks us to take a moment and reflect on someone who is still alive and helped us or said something that facilitated an improvement in our lives. This should be someone who was never properly thanked and we could also meet with in the near future. If we are stuck and can't think of anyone, we can try to think of a relative, teacher, colleague, or boss who may fit this description.

In his book, Seligman says, "Gratitude can make your life happier and more satisfying. When we feel gratitude, we benefit from the pleasant memory of a positive event in our life. Also, when we express our gratitude to others, we strengthen our relationship with them. But sometimes our thank you is said so casually or quickly that it is nearly meaningless. Your task is to write a letter of gratitude to this individual and deliver it in person. The letter should be concrete and about three hundred words: be specific about what she did for you and how it affected your life. Let her know what you are doing now, and mention how you often remember what she did. Make it sing."

Once the testimonial has been written, contact the person and set up a meeting but be vague about the purpose of this meeting. The exercise is more fun as a surprise. Finally, when the meeting occurs, take time reading the letter and enjoy the conversation this sparks with a potential deepening of the relationship.

After the meeting and the reading of the letter, Seligman says almost everyone cries tears of joy. Seligman says that if we partake in this activity, "You will be happier and less depressed one month from now."

─────────────────────────── ∞∞∞ ───────────────────────────

The Gratitude Letter in the Classroom

When this was implemented in our class, one student wrote a gratitude letter to one of the teachers in our school. The next time I saw that teacher, she had the biggest smile I have ever seen on her face. She told me that she was really struggling with work and some personal problems, but this letter helped her see how much she is making a difference in our students' lives.

At home, she posted the letter where she can see it when she gets ready every morning. This enables her to start the day off with a smile. In fact, this experience was so powerful, the teacher wrote a gratitude letter to a colleague to keep the gratitude chain going.

─────────────────────────── ∞∞∞ ───────────────────────────

REWIRING YOUR BRAIN FOR HAPPINESS

Another useful book that deepens our understanding of positive psychology is *Hardwiring Happiness: The New Brain Science of Contentment, Calm, and Confidence* by Dr. Rick Hanson. Like Seligman's book, this book draws on the latest research in the area of positive psychology. It is extremely inspiring to read about the mechanisms that enable us to be happier and actually change the hardwiring or neural pathways in our brains. Astonishingly, according to Hanson, this rewiring can take place in as little as three minutes a day. What a great investment of time!

In his book, Hanson writes that recent studies have shown that establishing some simple habits can facilitate this recalibration and restructuring in our brain. Behind this research is the idea of "neuroplasticity," which means the brain has the ability to alter and reshape its structure in response to life's experiences. This powerfully challenges the old idea that the brain is a static organ, that it is fixed and not easily changed, especially once we reach adulthood.

GRATITUDE RESHAPES OUR BRAINS

According to Dr. Hanson, the key to rewiring our brains is to focus and linger on positive experiences. We can build on these ideas from Hanson's book and see how gratitude lends itself to reflecting on the positive experiences in life. This is where the powerful tool of gratitude comes into play, helping to recalibrate our brains in fresh and positive ways. Accentuating the positive with gratitude may even allow us to turn an apparently negative experience into a positive one by reframing the experience through the lens of gratitude.

To get a better understanding of this topic, we may look at the brain as a forest and the paths through the forest that are used most often become permanent paths for the neural activity in our brains. Conversely, the paths that are infrequently used tend to disappear. So, repeatedly focusing on things we are grateful for in life allows us to transform our brain, making those positive paths stronger, more easily accessible, and making our view of the world more optimistic.

THE NEGATIVE BIAS

Supporting Seligman's earlier point that our brains have a built-in "negative bias," Hanson helps us understand that the evolutionally basis of negative thinking seems to be pre-programmed in our brains. Our brains have developed over the millennia to focus on any perceived threats to our survival, the most important thing to any organism.

Thus, the negative experiences that threatened survival got all the attention, like the fear of starving or being attacked. These negative emotions had staying power, whereas the pleasant or positive experiences could be forgotten quickly without affecting survival. Hanson writes, "Over the course of evolution, animals that were nervous, driven and clinging were more likely to pass on their genes, and their inclinations are now woven into our DNA. Even when you feel relaxed and happy and connected, your brain keeps scanning for potential dangers, disappointments, and interpersonal issues."

Even though today we may not need to focus so much on those negative things or be constantly scanning for imminent danger, our brains still have the tendency to do that. As Hanson puts it, our brains are naturally "Velcro" for the bad feelings, whereas our brains are more like "Teflon" for the positive experiences. This is where applying gratitude has the power to help overcome the negative bias and reshape our brains to feel more positive emotions.

Furthermore, Hanson gives us a present day example of the "negative bias." In life, we can have ten important experiences in a day: five will be positive, four will be neutral, and one will be negative. At the end of the day, or maybe on the drive home, what do we dwell on? Because of our natural negative tendency, that negative experience will be what we put our attention on and that will strengthen our negative feelings and general anxiety.

So, the big questions are, "How do we actually rewire our brain?" and "Does it take a lot of time or money?" Thankfully, there are some simple exercises that do not take much time or money, two commodities that usually seem to be in short supply. The key to rewiring our brains for happiness, according to Hanson, is to focus and build an awareness of the positive experiences, dwelling on them as they occur throughout the day. Here again, gratitude helps us see all the positive things happening to us. Taking an extra moment to absorb a positive experience, maybe ten seconds, allows the brain to build up those positive pathways.

HAPPINESS ACTIVITY

Now would be a good point to try out a happiness activity. Today, when we have a positive or pleasurable experience, like that first cup of coffee, a hot shower, or a hug from someone we love, take a deep breath and dwell on it, savor it. Maybe that sensation could be a delicious meal or hearing our favorite song, or simply enjoying the sunshine on a beautiful day. Practicing this simple activity begins the process that allows our brain to make those positive connections stronger in our brains.

Right now, let's try to think about something we have eaten recently that we have enjoyed. Imagine that flavor, whether it was a perfectly ripe peach, a warm chocolate chip cookie out of the oven, or a cool sip of ice tea on a hot day. Try to imagine the taste and the smell and feel the deep satisfaction that it brings our bodies.

At this point, we may bring gratitude into the equation by realizing the gift of this taste and everything that has come into play to bring this taste to our mouths, from growing the fruit or processing the tea, to transporting it to the store and getting it into our hands. We are given the opportunity to savor gratitude daily if we can remember to take time before we eat a meal or during the experience of eating.

BENEFITS OF PRACTICING GRATITUDE

We have looked at the background of positive psychology and the way we may reprogram our brains to experience more happiness. Now, let's look at some specific examples of research in the area of gratitude. Two researchers,

Dr. Emmons and Dr. McCullough, studied gratitude and found that people who practiced gratitude did not experience fewer problems in life. Instead, they found that subjects practicing gratitude did not let those problems bother them as much. This sense of strength and resilience seems to have been developed through their use of gratitude. They build up an ability to "reframe" problems in their lives and even see them as "challenges" that may help them grow.

The findings in this study have compelling implications for our lives. If we are able to look at life through the lens of gratitude, we then have the freedom to be happier. We do not have to wait for our problems or stresses to go away or diminish. We may take action and reduce our stress by practicing gratitude and becoming conscious of the good things in our lives right now. Through studies like these, we can see that we do not need life to get easier; we can become stronger, happier, and more resilient by utilizing gratitude in our lives.

Thus, we don't have to wait for a promotion at work or winning the lottery to be happy. We don't need to postpone living until that special person enters our lives or maybe even exits our lives. We can become conscious of all the good things and loving people in our lives right now and commence to be a little happier immediately. This is simple, but it is not always easy. It just takes perseverance and effort.

Overall Psychological Benefits of Gratitude

Positive psychology has empirically studied the psychological benefits of gratitude. These include:

- Lowering the risk of depression
- Reducing negative emotions like envy, regret, and resentment
- Overcoming trauma and improving mental resilience, even during hard times
- Lowering aggression and increasing empathy
- Improving self-esteem

Overall Physical Benefits of Gratitude

Moreover, developing an attitude of gratitude not only makes us happier and more psychologically "fit," but it can improve our health. Various studies have found positive benefits of gratitude for our physical health, including:

- Reducing stress hormones like cortisol by up to 23 percent
- Improving duration and quality of sleep
- Increasing white blood cells that help fight disease
- Making healthier choices, like avoiding smoking

Gratitude and the Study of Cardiac Medicine

Gratitude benefits are not limited to the area of positive psychology. New research in a variety of disciplines is extremely encouraging. Another area where we see the positive impact of practicing gratitude is in the study of cardiac medicine.

One recent study, presented at University of California, San Diego, Institute for Public Health's Annual Public Health Research Day in April 2015, focused on the benefits of applying gratitude to the field of behavioral cardiology. This field of cardiac medicine used to be focused on negative traits, like hostility, depression, and stress. But now, this field has turned to more positive psychology attributes, like gratitude, compassion, and empathy.

Remarkably, in this study, beginning a "gratitude journal" was shown as an effective resource for improving the struggles associated with the symptoms of heart failure. In a cross-sectional study on over 180 heart failure patients, the patients who practiced this gratitude activity in their lives exhibited less depression, better sleep, and even a positive physical benefit: less peripheral inflammation.

Furthermore, this study included a randomized clinical trial where patients were assigned to either eight weeks of gratitude journaling plus their usual care or eight weeks or usual care alone. Participants who kept the gratitude journal had increased heart rate variability, which is a measure of reduced cardiac risk.

In addition, these patients showed reduced circulating levels of inflammatory biomarkers IL-6 and sTNFr1, which are associated with cardiovascular disease. The physical benefit of keeping a gratitude journal furthers our understanding of the far-reaching positive impact of applying gratitude activities in our lives.

STEPPING STONES TO GRATITUDE

1. Positive psychology has turned from looking at the negative aspects of life to the positive, from "learned helplessness" to "learned optimism."
2. The study of gratitude and its application in our lives is a key component of positive psychology.
3. Simple gratitude activities, like recording gratitude or conducting a gratitude visit, may be employed to help us increase our happiness and improve our physical health.
4. Taking time to savor the positive experiences in life may help rewire our brains.

5. Subjects using a gratitude journal do not experience fewer problems in life, but they don't let those problems bother them as much.
6. Cardiac patients who utilized a gratitude journal had alleviated negative symptoms and improved cardiac health.

LET'S TALK ABOUT IT

1. Why did the study of psychology shift from focusing on negative aspects of psychology to positive?
2. What are some activities that have been studied and shown to positively impact people's lives?
3. Which activities in this chapter should we try in our lives to start practicing gratitude and enjoy the benefits it brings us?

Chapter Two

Challenge the
Culture of Complaining

Men are disturbed not by things, but by the view which they take of them.

—Epictetus

Change your thoughts and you change your world.

—Norman Vincent Peale

EXPLORING THE ROOTS OF DISSATISFACTION WITH LIFE

Before introducing gratitude to students, we can ask them to consider the opposite end of the spectrum: complaining. Specifically, ask them, "Why do people complain so much?" or a more relevant question, "Why do we still complain so much?" An honest answer is that it feels good to complain and blame someone or something else when things are not going our way. Complaining takes the responsibility off of us and often engenders the comforting response we crave when we fail or are disappointed.

The reason many people still complain is that for every behavior, there is a payoff. Sometimes, we are not aware of the payoff we are seeking and worse, the payoff can be more negative than positive. For example, sometimes we complain because we want others to commiserate with us, but we may be only bringing the other person down.

Furthermore, by complaining, we don't need to change anything about ourselves. Worse, we remain stuck and spread our toxic attitude to others. There is a fatal flaw to complaining, no matter what kind of temporary relief it may offer. When we feed each other's negativity, we sap our motivation to change and make the problems seem even more difficult than they are.

When we complain, at first we feel relief, but in the end, we turn into victims, powerless and depressed. Ultimately, we are not victims—we are volunteers. If we don't find a way to curtail this behavior, it becomes a pernicious habit that gets embedded into our worldview.

No Sourpusses Around Here

Recently, a fellow educator commented that their school is in the process of hiring new teachers and one of the unstated requirements for a candidate is that they must have the "ability to feel joy in the presence of teenagers." My colleague went on to say that it seems too common for teachers to jump on the bandwagon of exasperation and frustration, but their principal said, "We don't need another sourpuss around here."

HOW COMPLAINING BECAME ENDEMIC IN SCHOOL SETTINGS

Wherever we look in our schools, we can find negativity: in classrooms, hallways, offices, and teacher's lounges. Participating in such talk is easy because there is a lot "wrong" in our schools, but this kind of dialogue is destructive and often spreads quickly. The media is filled with stories about our failed schools, inept teachers, indifferent parents, and their unmotivated or distracted students. However, we can't blame the media for the culture of complaining in education. Let's explore how we may modify this caustic behavior.

CHANNELING COMPLAINTS

Complaining is different than healthy "venting." There's nothing wrong with speaking to a friend after a bad day and letting out all the negativity. Then, we can let it go. This is a way to channel that energy into a healthy behavior. Complaining is different. It is unhealthy and many people are unaware of just how much they practice this destructive habit.

Here is an example: Imagine that we are out at a restaurant and the waiter brings us the wrong order. Do we say nothing and eat it? No, we can say, "This is the wrong order. Would you please bring me the correct order?" However, if we are not watching our behavior, we would say something like,

"I can't believe how incompetent you are. What an awful restaurant this is. I'm never coming here again." Then, we would go home and post something on social media about the terrible experience at the restaurant. However, we always have a choice in how to respond in life. We can try to deal with a problem simply and appropriately or react blindly with complaining.

At school, if we are having problems with a student, parent, or colleague, what do we do? We can complain about them to others or we could do nothing, let it go on, and possibly escalate the situation. Conversely, we could go to a trusted friend or administrator and present the problem and ask for help. This is a positive way to channel that energy.

TURNING A NEGATIVE INTO A POSITIVE

Brian

During my first year of teaching, I had a wonderful friend named Brian. One day, I got a call, saying Brian was in the hospital in the intensive care unit. His appendix had burst, and he went to the emergency room. Unfortunately, he was misdiagnosed with a severely upset stomach and sent home. Sepsis set in and he almost died.

When I visited him in the hospital, I asked him how he was doing, and he said, "I am turning a negative into a positive." I thought, if there is one person who has a right to complain, it'd be Brian, who almost lost his life from a mistake. However, Brain went on to say that he had been working more than sixty hours per week and never spent time with his family. Now, he said that he would have time to spend with his family and get his priorities in order. His children around his hospital bed smiled as he said this.

This was an extremely powerful example that I share with my students. Brian reframed his experience by reflecting and looking deeper at what positive could come out of his negative experience. If Brian can find a way to turn his profoundly negative experience into a positive one, can't we all turn our little complaints and negative situations into positive solutions?

Another way to illustrate the concept of making this kind of turnaround is to tell our students a simple anecdote: A shoe salesman goes to a new country to expand his business and finds that no one wears shoes. At first, he sends a message to his boss saying, "No chance of expanding business here; no one wears shoes." After thinking about the situation again and trying to find a positive outlook in this apparently negative situation, he sends another message: "Tremendous opportunity to expand business here; no one wears shoes."

This story reminds students that it's not so much what happens in life, but how we see it through the filter of our attitude, especially as we actively prepare to implement gratitude in our classrooms and lives.

ELEVATING THE CULTURE IN OUR SCHOOLS

As teachers, sometimes we complain to colleagues or our principal about certain students. However, it is important to keep in mind a simple fact: sometimes good students make bad choices. This idea can change our attitude about our students and adjust our level of complaining. We can even apply this to people in general, saying, "That is a good person who just made a bad choice." This powerful idea makes it easier to forgive and keep an open door to restoring healthy relationships.

NO COMPLAINT ZONE

To promote a positive culture among teachers, we can suggest making the faculty lounge an area of "No Negativity." If someone starts complaining or talking negatively about someone who isn't in the room, we can gently remind that person in a neutral tone, "It is not fair to speak about that person when they cannot defend themselves."

This ground rule for the teacher's lounge creates a safe and supportive environment. Teachers may comment that they feel they've become more aware of how much they were complaining about others and they may start to change their behavior. With this ground rule in place, gossiping, as well as complaining, can be greatly curtailed.

A SIX PACK AND A SMILE

Another area to address is faculty meetings. Since faculty meetings can some-times degenerate into "complaining sessions," we can start each meeting with a "Six Pack and a Smile" by bringing a six pack of soda and asking teachers to share something positive going on at the school or in their classrooms. After someone shares, they get a soda. Surprisingly, this simple activity helps bring joy into potentially gloomy faculty meetings and sets a positive tone for the meeting.

Teachers may also take this idea into the classroom but may consider bringing in something other than soda to give students when they share something positive. This uplifting exercise is a fantastic way to start or end any school day. One colleague gives students a single Skittle for sharing something positive. It is astonishing to see how much one little Skittle can brighten a student's day and help brighten the atmosphere in the classroom.

PROMOTING A POSITIVE CLASSROOM CULTURE

As teachers, we set the climate in our classroom and sometimes without realizing, we may bring a negative attitude of complaining to our students. It is inevitable that our attitudes and actions are going to set a tone with the students and create a culture in our classroom that will affect everything we do. Complaining is toxic to our students and even spreads out to our colleagues, administrators, and parents. Of course, we all have bad days when we don't feel good and we can't always be upbeat. However, we can start to watch that attitude and use some of the tools in this book to redirect our attitudes and actions.

Moreover, when we cultivate our awareness and change our behavior, students begin to reflect on their attitudes and together, we change the culture of our classroom. This will invariably help learning throughout the school year, especially as the year wears on and it gets easier to slip into a negative, retrogressive groove. We can reshape our mental patterns and also lay a strong, positive foundation for our students with the following activities.

NO COMPLAINING IN THIS CLASSROOM

At the beginning of each school year, we can begin a dialogue about complaining and how it contributes to negative attitudes. We can ask the students if they have any ideas about keeping complaints out of the classroom. One powerful rule that has emerged in this discussion in our classroom is that no one (including the teacher) is allowed to complain. If someone does complain, they would be asked to say three positive things about whom or what they were complaining about.

Breaking Old Habits with a Complaint Bracelet

Unfortunately, some days it is easy to slip back into old habits and complain. One helpful tool to try to get back on track is a complaint bracelet on our right wrists. If we notice we are complaining, we have to take it off and put it on our left wrist for the rest of the day and restart the process the next day. If we go three weeks without complaining, we can be freer of this pernicious and reoccurring habit.

In reality, it may take more than three weeks to successfully learn a new habit. Nevertheless, it is a novel way to redirect our behavior. Don't be afraid to ask students to create an exercise to try to curtail complaints.

Check out www.acomplaintfreeworld.com. The website has some potent ideas to implement this strategy in the classroom, including some curriculum outlining the three-week program. It includes journal prompts and class discussions as well as a clever poster to put in your classroom.

THE COMPLAINT CHALLENGE

The Complaint Challenge is another way to redirect complaining behavior. The challenge involves living with a specific question for one day: "Can we go all day without complaining?" Students carry around a 3 × 5-inch card and write down any instance when they complain or even feel like complaining. Then, students write a gratitude statement or something positive on the other side of the index card. For many students, this action develops a new awareness they may utilize their entire lives as they cultivate the ability to choose a positive attitude in any situation.

For example, one student noted that he complained every night and never really thought about how often he said, "I hate doing my homework!" But then, as this experiment progressed, he turned this statement into a gratitude and wrote, "I am grateful I get to learn by doing my homework. It will help me get a good job someday."

Another student wrote that she did not like setting the table every night for dinner. When she flipped that to a gratitude statement, she started saying, "I get to eat dinner with a loving family and I am thankful for that."

As this experiment moves forward, if students feel the complaints coming back, they pull out the index card and read the gratitude. Overall, it does work when the students try it and keep the effort up.

INTO ACTION

Try the activities presented here to improve our lives, as well as promote a positive culture in our classrooms and school. We can even spread it to the families of our students. Tell the students and their families about the effort.

It can even be fun. If we do complain, don't give up. Remember that being aware of a bad habit is the first step in changing it.

Whenever possible, turn the complaint into a gratitude statement. When we string together a few days without complaining, we will notice some other positive things going on, like our relationships improving and feeling more energy to put into teaching. We may even find we are enjoying life a little more.

In conclusion, it is truly astonishing to think how much time and energy we can waste with complaining. If we can go a few weeks without complaining (this is difficult, so just keep trying), we are well on our way to establishing a new and powerful habit that will serve us in our classrooms as well as in our lives. Trying to change this habit may seem daunting. Don't worry. Look for progress and not perfection. We can do this. *We can make the change.*

STEPPING STONES TO GRATITUDE

1. Complaining is toxic to us and everyone around us.
2. We complain for the payoff it brings, even if the payoff is negative.
3. We can turn negatives into positives by reflecting and then reframing our experience.
4. Try a complaint bracelet or take the Complaint Challenge to cultivate awareness of our behavior and then change it.
5. Be patient—look for progress and not perfection.

LET'S TALK ABOUT IT

1. Why do we complain so much?
2. What are some activities we can try to curtail our own complaining?
3. What can we do in our classrooms to help students become aware of complaining and then change this behavior to become more positive?

Chapter Three

Gratitude versus Materialism and Entitlement

The aim of life is appreciation; there is no sense in not appreciating things; and there is no sense in having more of them if you have less appreciation of them.

—G.K. Chesterton

FOCUSED ON MATERIALISM

Today, our society seems more focused on materialism than ever. Some of the reasons for this are evident. We are bombarded with messages from a variety of sources that say that if we just get enough of the "right" material things, we will be happy and content forever. Materialism seems to perpetuate itself as we tire of the latest acquisition and move on to the next thing that will fulfill us. Sadly, happiness is fleeting when we are on this "materialism treadmill."

Colleagues, administrators, and parents agree that one of the biggest areas of concern for our students is that sometimes they appear to be more focused on "things" and not as focused on building other aspects of their lives, like academic, social, and character skills.

Humorously, a good friend talks about participating in "retail therapy" and says succinctly, "Buying the perfect dress on sale brings complete happiness for about eight hours." Another friend recounts shopping excursions as a child to the local mall with her family when her mom would laugh and say, "People who say money doesn't buy happiness just don't know where to shop." This message that we may pass on to our children and students promulgates some of the materialism that pervades our society.

Nevertheless, we can also give our students and children another way to look at the world and a different way to live. Gratitude can help alleviate and realign these priorities. When we bring our attention to this issue and then try some of the activities listed in this chapter, we can start the process of countering the pernicious effects of materialism and entitlement.

MATERIALISM RESEARCH

Currently, materialism appears especially evident in our children and students with so many chances to partake in our consumer society. A strong body of research supports the idea that materialism does not bring sustained happiness. Specifically, research from Dr. Marcia Richins and Dr. Scott Dawson maintains the notion that materialistic people are less happy or satisfied with life than their peers. In another study from the *Journal of Personality and Social Psychology*, researchers go on to show that materialistic people suffer higher levels of depression, anxiety, and drug abuse.

What can parents and teachers do to change this rising tide of entitlement and materialism? Embracing and practicing gratitude has been shown to remedy some of the deleterious effects of materialism and entitlement. Gratitude gives us a new way of seeing the world and connecting us to other people, instead of negatively tying ourselves to "things" that make us happy.

Early research on materialism dates back to the 1990s, when Dr. Marcia Richins and Dr. Scott Dawson established the first scale to accurately measure materialism. In their study published in the *Journal of Consumer Research*, people who scored high on this scale were focused on acquiring things and saw these possessions as integral to their happiness.

Not surprisingly, over the past twenty years, people who scored high on this materialism scale scored lower on scales that measure happiness. Furthermore, Richins and Dawson discovered that materialistic people were less satisfied with their lives overall, as well as experiencing less enjoyment in daily activities.

Other researchers have looked specifically at materialism and gratitude, or rather, the lack of gratitude. In 2014, Jo-Ann Tsang and her colleagues from Baylor University published a study in the *Journal of Personality and Individual Differences*. In this study, Tsang surveyed over two hundred undergraduate students to determine their levels of materialism, gratitude, and life satisfaction. A compelling finding was that as the level of materialism increased, life satisfaction and gratitude plummeted. Upon further examination, one of the main things lacking for the more materialistic subjects was gratitude.

In what regards are materialism and gratitude diametrically opposing forces? Gratitude focuses on the positive aspects of life and the people that make those good things possible. Conversely, materialism focuses on the "things" we think we need that will bring us happiness. Inevitably, these expectations go unmet and we get back on the "materialism treadmill," getting more things, but enjoying them less. In a compelling study from 2009, Dr. Nathaniel Lambert was able to show that increasing gratitude actually helped lower levels of materialism.

GRATITUDE VERSUS ENTITLEMENT

Along with materialism, a related challenge many families and schools face currently is the sense that students feel more "entitled" than ever. Let's begin with a definition of *entitlement* given by the American Psychiatric Association as "unreasonable expectations of especially favorable treatment." How does entitlement relate to gratitude? The two are opposites. The paradox of entitlement is that when we always get what we want, we may appreciate it less.

However, there is some good news about entitlement. We have tools to combat entitlement and replace it with gratitude. Practicing gratitude in our schools and families can retrain our brains to help instill new actions, thinking, and a fresh perspective on life. Let's take a look at some possible roots of this sense of entitlement.

THE ORIGINS OF ENTITLEMENT

Often, entitlement is linked with expectations. In a humorous scene from Harry Potter that my son read recently, expectations are beautifully exemplified as Dudley, Harry's spoiled cousin, is counting his birthday presents and instead of being thankful, he erupts in anger when he notices that he didn't get as many gifts as he did the year before.

Likewise, in life sometimes we build up expectations of what we should get and if we don't get it as quickly as we like, we also may be upset. As parents and educators, our reactions to life show our students and children how to act, whether we realize it or not. Thus, our responses to the frustrations of not getting what we want as quickly as we want it gives our children and students a wrong example of how to act.

At least in some part, we are to blame for the sense of entitlement this young generation exhibits. Our out-of-proportion reactions and our willingness to give in to our children's demands may contribute to this. It seems that some act like parenting is a competition and this means supplying children with the latest and greatest of everything. Furthermore, others feel we are protecting our children and students in difficult situations when we are actually depriving them of experiencing the consequences of their actions.

Recently, Dr. Christine Carter wrote a humorous and ironic blog that warns us of the possible consequences of our parenting choices. Teachers and parents will find this very thought provoking.

Eleven Ways to Raise a Child Who is Entitled and Rude

1. *Make sure your kids have access to all the latest iDevices anytime they want. For example, they can be playing games on an iPad in the car while you are chauffeuring them around. That way, they won't even respond when you ask them about school or point out something interesting to them. (They won't even know where they are, or where they are going, and so they won't ask you those annoying "Are we there yet?" questions! You'll probably have to nag them to get out of the car they'll like being there so much!) Similarly, if they have their phone at dinner, they won't ever have to stop texting their friends, or engage in dinner table conversation—and so they will never be bored or antsy!*

2. *Do everything within your power to prevent your kids from feeling pain. This includes any sort of discomfort, difficulty, or disappointment. Cover for them when they make mistakes. Insist teachers raise mediocre grades. That way, kids won't learn how to rise to challenges or handle their mistakes themselves, and they will feel entitled to a life free from discomfort or disappointment. And when the going gets rough in the future, they'll be more likely to find a way to lie or cheat their way out of the situation—or they'll instantly start blaming others.*

3. *When things aren't going your way, point to the shortcomings of other people. You are entitled to good service from the dry cleaners, cable guy, flight attendants, etc. Since your kids will never have one of these jobs (see tip ten), there is really no need to show empathy or compassion toward underperforming service workers. Similarly, when your kids bring home bad grades, listen earnestly to their accusations about how bad their teachers are. Consider complaining to the principal or school head, or at least send an angry email. (Note: This strategy makes it likely that your kids will also complain harshly about you, which can be an excellent way to get in touch with your own shortcomings.)*

4. *Give them money whenever they need it. This is easier than remembering to dole out allowance, helping them find a job, teaching them to manage their own money, or helping them understand the relative cost of all the things they desperately "need."*

5. *Pay for as many enrichment activities, tutors, and the best sports teams you can afford. When you pay a lot for something, the coaches, faculty, and staff tend to feel they owe kids more success, praise, higher scores, trophies, etc. They are also more likely to go out of their way to ensure that your kids have a good time—and that they never feel defeated or disappointed.*

6. *Give your kids a break, especially if they (or you) aren't feeling well. Everyone is under a lot of pressure these days. It is okay to limit kids' video game playing or YouTube watching to two hours a day, for example, but these rules can be ridiculously hard to enforce on a day-to-day basis, much less if anything out of the ordinary is happening. If you think they might have a sore throat, or if they seem too tired to go to school, let them stay home and watch Netflix or ESPN all day—especially if they don't like school very much.*

7. *Refuse to consistently enforce bedtimes. It is normal for kids to want to stay up late, especially if they are texting with their friends or there is a big game on TV. One night, nag them until they go to bed. The next night, you'll likely all be tired from the previous night's effort, so just let them choose their own bedtime, or ignore them until they fall asleep on their own. That way they will realize that, actually, they are in control of their bedtimes. If their attention or impulse control at school suffers because they are tired, excellent stimulants, like Ritalin, are widely available.*

8. *Confide in your kids as though they are your close friends, especially if you really need someone to talk to about a problem or if you are already crying or enraged. Lack of boundaries creates the expectation that your business is their business to worry about and fix. Having you as a friend first and parent second ensures that their close friendships with peers don't fully develop, and therefore won't interfere with their closeness to you (or their ability to support you when you need them). Moreover, this lack of boundaries will ensure that they are often rude to you, much in the same way they are with their siblings.*

9. *Don't insist kids write thank you notes. Kids are busy, and so are you (and we all know it is you that will be saddled with addressing and mailing the notes). People already know that kids are grateful for all they have and everything that receive; no need for them to learn how to express their appreciation in written form, especially given how much they already have going on.*

10. *Make sure they never have to do an entry-level or minimum wage job. Boredom is uncomfortable and unnecessary (see tip two). Working their way up in an organization is a waste of time if you can use your connections to help them start at the top; hopefully they'll pick up a strong work ethic from all the people around them that did earn their positions. (If they need cash, see tip four.) Bonus #1: Kids start to assume that all adults are willing to go the extra mile for them, and that they are entitled to skip the hard bits in life. Bonus #2: This will greatly reduce the odds that they'll ever work in a service industry, or have the chance to work alongside people different from them—and increase the odds that they'll act superior and degrading to servers and cashiers everywhere.*

11. *Above all, let them out of their chores around the house. Kids often have trouble managing their time; it is understandable if they are distracted by video games, Instagram, or ten thousand texts from their friends. Nothing is more relevant to adolescents than what is happening on their phones— remember, this is normal. They need to keep up with the social scene if they are to have friends and be accepted by their peer group. If they have*

homework, don't compound their distraction or time-management issues by asking them to empty the dishwasher.

These techniques will ensure not just that your kid will be ill-mannered and entitled, but also possibly insecure, materialistic, anxious (or arrogant), and dependent. They definitely won't develop the skills they need to sustain lasting and loyal friendships without your near constant interference, to handle stress and anxiety without drugs and alcohol, or to hold down a real job without your connections. What better way to shore up our family connections than to ensure that our kids always live with us?

Does this post make you cringe? It makes me a little nervous because I have done nearly all of these things myself at some point as a parent! But then I remember that we are parenting in a culture that makes it very easy to make these mistakes! Even so, we can raise kind kids with strong characters.

POSITIVE DISCIPLINE

In our classrooms, we can instill a "positive discipline" system that helps students learn from their mistakes and may help keep them from developing those feelings of entitlement. At the beginning of every year in our class, when explaining the "positive" discipline system we use, we tell the students that we will not punish them, but we will allow them to experience the consequences of their action. The difference between punishment and consequences becomes evident when they see that they have the power to choose the correct action and get a positive consequence or they can choose a negative action and get an adverse consequence.

Allowing the consequences to follow the action helps the students pair their action with what naturally happens. If a student does not do his or her homework, it is important that he or she gets a consequence, like a lower grade, so the student will actually complete it next time. Sometimes, a parent may try to get the student out of this consequence with an excuse, instead of allowing it to happen. However, by experiencing the possibly painful consequence, we are encouraging the student to reshape their behavior.

GRATITUDE—A RESPONSE TO ENTITLEMENT

Applying gratitude in our classrooms and families is another powerful step to displace entitlement. When we employ one of the gratitude strategies in our schools and families, we are allowing a new way of thinking and acting to form. Nevertheless, this change doesn't always happen quickly. We need to be patient and realize we are trying to supersede some entrenched habits of thinking and acting.

WRITE A THANK YOU CARD

Another simple yet effective tool to help combat entitlement with gratitude is to have children write a "Thank You" card when they receive a present, when someone does something nice for them, or even to thank someone for being a friend. A handwritten card is more effective because it is more personal, sincere, and shows that a person is willing to take more time in the endeavor. In addition, sending it by traditional mail also gives it some novelty in our increasing technological world of communication.

As teachers and parents, we can model this behavior and show our children and students the "Thank You" cards and notes we send to our friends and family. This is an activity we can start early and even allow the younger children to draw their "Thank You" instead of writing it.

GRATEFUL GIVING DISPLACING ENTITLEMENT

Gratitude and altruism go hand in hand. When students feel more grateful, they are more likely to want to reciprocate by helping others. Then, in the act of giving, those feelings of entitlement are replaced with the joy of helping others.

In the same way we practice gratitude in the classroom, we can make gratitude an action in our students' families, showing that it is more than merely a pleasant feeling. Transforming gratitude from a feeling to an action can sometimes be a challenge. But giving as a family provides an opportunity for altruistic actions. There are many ways and opportunities to give, as shown in the vignettes that follow in this chapter. Practiced as a family, grateful giving can help displace feelings of entitlement. One friend put it succinctly, "Don't tell me how grateful you are—show me how grateful you are."

One of the true gifts of encouraging students to practice gratitude is when we see gratitude propel them to altruistic actions, like this next vignette. Helping others is one of the most effective ways to dispel entitlement, and Joseph is a perfect example.

Joseph

The first year I taught fourth grade, I had an exceptional student named Joseph. He demonstrated an integrity that stood out, even among the naturally honest students. Adding gratitude to his character traits through the school year, I knew Joseph was going to be an outstanding person.

Over the years, it had been my pleasure to keep in touch with Joseph and see that he did become an extraordinary young man. He entered college this year and got in touch with me the other day saying, "Mr. Griffith, I have to tell you

*what I did today. Today I helped three homeless people." I told him that was
wonderful and it didn't surprise me, but made me feel grateful. I wanted to hear
the story of what happened and what prompted this selfless act.*

*He said he was driving home and saw three homeless men and just felt like
he should talk to them and see if he could help them. A powerful storm was
predicted for later that day and he wanted to get them to safety. The men said
they did indeed need help and asked if they could hop into the back of his truck.*

*Joseph said, "Yes, get in" and proceeded to drive them to a local church, but
the church said they did not have the facilities to take in three homeless men.
This did not deter Joseph; he checked local resources and found a homeless
shelter nearby. He got the men some water and even took them to McDonalds
before dropping them off. One man had a sad story of getting drunk on vodka
and finding himself on the streets. Another talked about trying to find his wife
who was last reported in a local homeless shelter.*

*One of the men asked if he could have the shoes off Joseph's feet, but he put
up a healthy boundary here, saying, "I am a poor college student and I need my
shoes." I told Joseph that was a reasonable response, and that the shelter could
get them some shoes. Our school has done some work with this shelter and they
do gladly provide those kinds of resources.*

*I asked Joseph what prompted this action and he said that he saw these
guys and felt a profound gratitude for all he had. This deep sense of gratitude
prompted Joseph to help them. Not wanting any notoriety for this altruistic act,
Joseph requested that I didn't tell anyone else, but the story exemplified the action of gratitude, so I asked him if I could use it in this book and he said that I
could, if it would help other people.*

*Finally, Joseph asked if I had any advice for him and I told him that I was
extremely proud of him and his action, but next time he should get a friend to
help him in this kind of action to ensure his safety and also to give a friend an
opportunity to enjoy the benefits of an altruistic act.*

WAYS TO PRACTICE ALTRUISM

Coming from a foundation of gratitude, families can undertake acts of altruism and compassion to foster gratitude and overtake feelings of entitlement. Moreover, by demonstrating gratitude as a family, we are helping to
recalibrate our priorities and to eliminate those overpowering feelings of
privilege. Finding an organization to contribute to as a class or as a family
and also volunteering are powerful steps in helping gratitude eclipse feelings
of privilege. Even volunteering a few hours a month can help bring about
the desired change.

Here are two exceptional examples of students demonstrating gratitude with their family and bringing their unselfish actions to help others.

———————————————————————— ∞ ————————————————————————

Leah

In our class, one girl had a clever and effective method of saving money so she could then donate to a worthy cause. With the help of her family, she kept three piggy banks and when she earned money or was given money, she would divide it up evenly between the "Saving Jar," "Spending Jar," and "Giving Jar." She decided to research charities and then donate the money from her "Giving Jar" to an organization that she believed in.

The organization she decided to support resulted partly from my own family situation, which I have shared with my class. My son, Asher, was born in Ethiopia, and it was our extraordinary pleasure to adopt him. He is the light of our lives. He is now six years old and reading books to me as he finishes kindergarten. He and I compose songs in our music room together and he calls our "rock band" the Electric Stars, even getting my wife involved sometimes. We also compose gratitude lists together.

When Leah heard about Asher, she said she wanted to help other children in Ethiopia and Africa. As a class, we found a couple who started an organization that gives African orphans formula and baby blankets. The parents of students helped organize a party to make blankets for the orphans. They used some of the money that Leah and other students had saved to purchase formula as well as inviting other people to donate to the cause. By the cutoff date for donations, we were able to get the blankets and baby formula to many Ethiopian school children.

With any of these endeavors, it is also important to follow-up and see how the donations have helped reshape lives. This keeps the students less concerned about their own material possessions and more focused on how they can help others. With the Ethiopia project, we received cards sent by the orphanage workers, writing about how many babies' lives we were able to help. At the end of this project, Leah gave a report on Ethiopian orphans and even said she hoped to grow up and adopt a baby from Ethiopia someday.

One of the truly powerful aspects of altruistic action is to see our students light up with a new joy as they try to make a difference in someone else's life. The new sense of empowerment builds in the students as they watch the profound change that they can bring. One student said, "I never realized that making blankets and sending them to Ethiopia could make me feel so good about myself. I feel connected to some other students from the other side of the world that I never even knew about."

———————————————————————— ∞ ————————————————————————

This next vignette is one of my favorites because Sabrina used Leah's idea and developed it further.

--- ☊ ---

Sabrina

Sabrina, with the help of her family, started an online organization to raise money for orphans around the world. She came into school one day with the most joyful smile I have ever seen on her face. She asked, "Mr. Griffith, can I share something with the class?" I told her that she could at the end of morning work.

Throughout the morning I could see her squirming in her seat, almost ready to burst with the excitement of what she had to tell us. When it came time, she got up and said, "This year has been so amazing and I really believe in helping the orphans of the world, so I started a charity on the Internet to help those kids."

Surprised and impressed, a student asked her to tell us how she accomplished this. She explained how she got the idea one day one her way home, after seeing the photos of the Ethiopian students that we had helped. Then, she took the inspiration to her family. She knew that her dad, who worked with computers, could help her get it going. So Sabrina and her father set up a crowdfunding site, with the funds going to the charity to help orphans.

Helping others is one thing, but creating a new charity to support numerous others is astonishing, a real example of gratitude in action. But really, we shouldn't be surprised: our students have these ideas within them, we just need to give them space to open them up and allow it to come out.

--- ☊ ---

Finally, here is a story from my family about helping others, practicing gratitude, and what we learned from the endeavor.

--- ☊ ---

Making Care Kits for the Homeless

Last Christmas, our neighbors had the creative and powerful idea to make little "survival" kits for homeless people. The idea was that our two families would get together and make a list of the things that should be in these kits. Next, we would split the list and purchase the items. Finally, we would have a little party where we would talk about the joy of helping others as our children helped us assemble the kits.

In these kits, my son thought everyone should have a toothbrush and soap, so they would feel clean. We also inserted protein bars because our neighbor's daughter said that when she was hungry and away from home, a protein bar always made her tummy feel better. So, we proceeded to put the kits together in a big box and took them to the local homeless shelter.

As we undertook this activity, we wove in gratitude, talking about how fortunate we are to have a house, where we feel safe and can take a shower anytime we want. Also, we expressed our thankfulness for all the food we have at our fingertips and the fact that we never really have to feel hungry.

This activity had some far-reaching positive results. The next time we ventured into downtown Atlanta to visit the zoo, our son saw a homeless person and said, "Look, there is one of the homeless people we helped. Can we do that again to help more people?" Of course we will do that again and bring more gratitude into our lives while helping others.

By promoting and practicing gratitude, we have the opportunity to displace feelings of entitlement and materialism with positive actions. This may not happen overnight, so just keep trying and celebrate the little victories.

STEPPING STONES TO GRATITUDE

1. Materialism does not bring happiness. In fact, research shows that the more materialistic we are, the less happy we become.
2. The opposite of gratitude is entitlement, and practicing gratitude as a family may help overcome those feelings of privilege.
3. Families may utilize acts of altruism, along with gratitude, to displace feelings of entitlement by encouraging children to volunteer, contribute to charities, or start an organization for a worthy cause.
4. Putting our gratitude into action as a family can change our children, our families, and our world.

LET'S TALK ABOUT IT

1. Why does our society seem more materialistic than ever?
2. What does the research say about materialism as it relates to happiness and gratitude?
3. What is the opposite of gratitude?
4. What are some things we can do to help students become more grateful and less materialistic and entitled?

Chapter Four

Overcoming Barriers to Gratitude

I hate ingratitude more in a man than lying, vainness, babbling, drunken-
ness, Or any taint of vie whose strong corruption inhabits our frail blood.

—William Shakespeare,
from *Twelfth Night, or, What You Will* (Viola at III, iv)

An old saying goes, "A rising tide floats all boats." As this quote so articu-
lately conveys, if we have a rising tide of gratitude in our classrooms, families, or schools, everyone benefits. Then, we may ask, why isn't everyone
open to gratitude? A number of reasons exist that may explain why gratitude
isn't always embraced.

Some of the biggest barriers to gratitude are misconceptions people have
about gratitude. We will start with some general myths and misconceptions
about gratitude, and we will debunk them with scientific research. Then, we
will examine some specific barriers to gratitude in the classroom and the
means to work through them.

DEBUNKING MYTHS THAT BLOCK GRATITUDE

Dr. Robert Emmons, a pioneering gratitude researcher, published a paper in
November 2013 on The Greater Good Center for Science website that examined some myths about gratitude. Applying the latest scientific research, Emmons takes a fresh look at this subject. All these misconceptions are barriers
to enjoying gratitude and unfortunately keep people from utilizing this powerful tool in their lives and classrooms. But, as we understand these obstacles
and look at the reality and the scientific research, we are paving the way for
implementing gratitude and reaping the rewards that come with embracing it.

MYTH ONE: GRATITUDE LEADS TO COMPLACENCY

The first myth, according to Emmons, is that gratitude leads to complacency. On the contrary, gratitude empowers people to achieve their goals. In research conducted by Dr. Emmons and colleagues, they found that subjects who kept a gratitude journal as well as listing goals were 20 percent closer to achieving those goals than the group that did not take part in the gratitude activity.

Moreover, Emmons goes on to say, "This finding does not surprise me because people made to keep a gratitude journal in my studies consistently report feeling more energetic, alive, awake, and alert. Yet they don't report feeling more satisfied with their progress toward their goals than other people do. They don't become complacent or satisfied to the point that they stop making an effort."

As educators, we are constantly striving in the classroom to become better teachers as well as helping our students achieve their goals. By implementing gratitude in our lives and the lives of our students, we are getting closer to attaining those goals and as this research suggests, gratitude may help us generate more energy and motivation as we progress toward our goals.

MYTH TWO: GRATITUDE IS JUST POSITIVE THINKING

Unfortunately, some educators dismiss gratitude as too "touchy-feely." One colleague even went so far as to say gratitude was just another "Kum-Bah-Yah" activity. Both of these opinions echo the idea that gratitude is just a naïve form of positive thinking. However, gratitude is so much more than just positive thinking or a pleasant feeling. Gratitude is a way of interacting with life, a way of openly receiving all the gifts we are given and giving credit to those who provide them.

Moreover, being grateful does not mean ignoring negative aspects of life. As Emmons so eloquently puts it, "Practicing gratitude magnifies positive feelings more than it reduces negative feelings. If it was just positive thinking, or just a form of denial, you'd experience no negative thoughts or feelings when you're keeping a gratitude journal, for instance. But, in fact, people do. So gratitude isn't just a nice, warm, fuzzy feeling."

MYTH THREE: GRATITUDE ISN'T POSSIBLE WHEN WE ARE SUFFERING

An additional misconception about gratitude is that it is not possible to be grateful when we are experiencing adversity or suffering in our lives. On the contrary, one of the truly powerful results of practicing gratitude is the resilience it gives us to get through adversity; gratitude enables us to keep perspective when we are going through challenging times. The hope that comes from gratitude helps us from being too overwhelmed by the setbacks in life.

A fascinating study concerning this myth was conducted by Dr. Philip Watkins and published in the *Journal of Positive Psychology*. In the study, Watkins and colleagues had subjects think of an unpleasant and unresolved memory where they may have been hurt or betrayed. Divided into three groups, the subjects were then asked to write about the experience. One group wrote about the positive aspects of the unsettling experience. Those who wrote from this grateful perspective didn't ignore or deny the negative aspects of the memory, but they articulated less unpleasant emotions than the other subjects and reported feeling more resilience and closure.

In further research, Dr. Emmons asked people suffering from severe neuromuscular disease to keep a gratitude journal for two weeks. The group who kept a gratitude journal reported the following results:

• More positive emotions
• More optimism about upcoming events
• More connected to others (even though many lived alone)
• Getting more restful sleep

Poison Ivy

Not all of life's challenging situations are easy to welcome with open arms. Once while gardening, I got a severe case of poison ivy. Even with medicine, I had painful outbreaks. A friend laughed and said, "I would like to see you find some gratitude in having poison ivy." Quickly, I said that I am grateful that I will know how to identify poison ivy so I won't get it next time, but he dismissed that. He gave me a week to come up with a deeper gratitude. I didn't know if I was up for the challenge, but when I try to grow with gratitude, I am always rewarded somehow.

The next day, while standing in line to check out at store I caught a woman looking at my poison ivy outbreak with such disgust that it made me feel like a leper. She didn't see me look at her, but I got a little taste of how it feels to be stared at because of a physical ailment.

My poison ivy cleared up after two long weeks, but that feeling will stay with me forever and I will have more compassion when I see or meet someone with any physical challenges. Finally, I got back to my friend and told him my gratitude, "Poison ivy enabled me to have more compassion for others." He agreed that I had passed the challenge.

MYTH FOUR: GRATITUDE MAKES
US TOO SELF-EFFACING

Another myth about gratitude, according to Emmons, is that gratitude makes us give all the credit for our success to others. Thus, we may risk overlooking our own accomplishments, hard work, or innate abilities. Dr. Emmons debunks this myth by saying, "Grateful people give credit to others, but not at the expense of acknowledging their own responsibility for their success. They take credit, too. It's not either/or—either I did this all myself or somebody else did it for me. Instead, they recognize their own feats and abilities while also feeling gratitude toward the people—parents, teachers—who helped them along the way."

TEACHERS' MISCONCEPTIONS ABOUT GRATITUDE

At this point, let's look specifically at misconceptions that teachers may hold toward gratitude. One general misconception some teachers have expressed is that gratitude is merely a pleasant feeling and is not applicable in educational settings. Gratitude is much more than a feeling; it is a way of teaching, thinking, and acting. Gratitude is a way of interacting with the world and seeing all the gifts we are given, as well as those responsible for the gifts.

Another misconception some teachers have is that we are born with a fixed disposition, and thus we are either grateful or not so grateful. Furthermore, this thinking goes on to say that we cannot do much to change our disposition or the disposition of our students. In addition, some have said that it is too hard to be grateful, that it is not their personality.

The research is interesting on this topic. Sonja Lyubomirsky, a psychology professor from the University of California, Riverside, writes about the "happiness set point," in her book, *The How of Happiness*. Lyubomirsky says that about 50 percent of our happiness is pre-set or genetic in a "happiness set point." Surprisingly, only 10 percent of our happiness comes from our "life circumstances." Finally, the remaining 40 percent comes from our outlook or our attitude.

Thus, we control 40 percent of how happy and how grateful we are. Lyubomirsky goes on to say that we can increase our happiness by practicing gratitude, optimism, and other acts of kindness. This is good news for all of us. We all can increase our happiness by intentionally practicing gratitude, no matter what our genetically "happiness set point" or our life circumstances.

MORE BARRIERS FOR
TEACHERS AND MORE SOLUTIONS

Additionally, some teachers have voiced the objection that they just do not have enough time to implement gratitude activities. As educators, we are constantly under pressure to get many things done daily. It seems like more and more is being added to an already impacted schedule. But some gratitude activities take a surprisingly short amount of time and are still potent classroom exercises.

Initially, we may need to devote about thirty minutes when introducing a gratitude activity, like completing a gratitude journal. Then, if we do this a couple times a week, it may take five minutes each time for a total of ten minutes from the week.

Another means of utilizing gratitude in the classroom without infringing on time constraints is to embed the gratitude activity within other subjects. For example, an English teacher can make writing a gratitude letter a writing assignment. For technology class, students can look for new gratitude activities online or study the latest developments in gratitude research.

As the school year progresses, we see that practicing gratitude in the classroom not only raises classroom culture, but imparts other skills to students, like increasing their connection to others. Additionally, this small investment in time helps our students deal with life and all its stresses in a resilient manner. The dividends this creates for a more positive classroom culture are priceless.

OVERCOMING THE BARRIERS TO GRATITUDE

How can we work through some of these obstacles and help others get over these impediments? Looking at the latest scientific research is a good way to start to overcome any hindrances to using gratitude. Not only does the research confirm that gratitude works in the classroom, it also offers activities and tools. Check the appendix in this book to investigate the latest research.

Also, feel free to share stories from this book about the benefits gratitude brings to educators, students, and their families. Hopefully, as we practice gratitude with our students and in our schools, we can add our own personal stories and positive outcomes when practicing gratitude.

WHY DOESN'T EVERYONE USE GRATITUDE?

Interestingly, one teacher said, "If gratitude is such a powerful and simple tool to apply to the classroom, why doesn't everyone do it?" Well, gratitude is simple, but may not be easy. Some teachers start trying their own gratitude activities, only to give up after a few days when they get too busy. Almost everyone who has persevered with gratitude has seen a positive influence in their lives and the lives of their students.

Another type of gratitude resistor may be the teacher that gets excited, tries to implement gratitude activities, but when the initial bubble pops and it doesn't bring the results quickly or as dramatically as hoped, he or she goes back to old behavior. One solution here is to give teachers, as well as students, "gratitude partners" to help encourage and keep everyone accountable for sticking with gratitude activities. Giving teachers "gratitude partners" will help this endeavor be more successful, as well as more fun.

Introducing something new for the classroom, even something as simple as this, sometimes does meet resistance. Having a partner share the successes and challenges helps educators get through initial opposition. Furthermore, if a "check-in" is established, when gratitude partners can briefly meet each week for five to ten minutes, long-term success is much more likely.

CREATING BUY-IN FROM ALL STAKEHOLDERS

To overcome these obstacles to gratitude implementation in a school, we also should try to get everyone in the school on board with this new teaching tool. This may be a challenge, but it is worth making the effort. The administration may begin this process by introducing gratitude and its activities at a meeting or training session.

To help jump start gratitude integration at the school, the principal may even give a short gratitude activity. One example of such an activity is to have teachers write a gratitude statement about someone else in the school on small pieces of paper, saying why they are grateful for that person. Then, pass out the notes to the recipients, helping everyone feel the immediate results of practicing gratitude. A simple activity like this can get the ball rolling for the school in a positive and powerful manner.

Then, show the teachers what gratitude in the classroom may look like. Fantastic videos are available online, showing gratitude being implemented successfully in the classroom with a variety of activities. Check the appendix for links.

Another option is to establish a gratitude group, where teachers can share their experiences, helping establish support, as well as making application of the new gratitude activities more successful. This could be part of grade-level groups already established or this could be an opportunity to start "Professional Learning Community" that investigates teaching tools, like gratitude.

At our school, a small gratitude group has been meeting weekly for over five years with tremendous results that reach far beyond the participants in the group.

Finally, teachers may be given a "gratitude curriculum" that helps them align the new activities with their current curriculum. In this curriculum, activities and supporting material are presented to make implementation as easy as possible. Effective online gratitude curriculums are available. Again, check the appendix for resources.

STUDENT MISCONCEPTIONS

Depending on their age, students may have many of the misconceptions that have been mentioned already. In addition, some students equate gratitude with the obligation of saying "Thank you" even when they don't feel it. In other words, some students think gratitude means just being polite.

Although being polite is important and should be encouraged, obligation is not the deeper gratitude we are trying to practice with these activities. It is important to distinguish between the external actions, like forcing a child say "Thank you," and truly practicing gratitude in our lives. True gratitude takes more effort, but the students will enjoy it more if they are given the chance to explore it. As mentioned earlier in the book, by introducing a gratitude curriculum, we are allowing students to delve deeper and see the costs and benefits of gratitude.

When we take time to examine and then dispel all these barriers to gratitude, we are helping construct a more positive culture in each classroom and in the entire school. After the barriers to gratitude have been addressed and overcome, it is truly empowering to see teachers, administrators, students, and staff welcome gratitude and allow it to mold their school and their lives in a positive manner.

STEPPING STONES TO GRATITUDE

1. Although gratitude is simple, it may not be easy for everyone.
2. Misconceptions and myths about gratitude prevent some people from trying gratitude.
3. By investigating and presenting the latest scientific research, misconceptions may be dispelled.

4. Educators may be resistant to implementation of gratitude for a number of reasons, but by trying to create school-wide support, application will be more successful.
5. Students may feel that gratitude is merely an obligation, but by introducing a gratitude curriculum they reach a deeper level of practicing gratitude.
6. After these obstacles are overcome, gratitude will help shape classes and an entire school in a new and positive manner.

LET'S TALK ABOUT IT

1. What are some myths about gratitude we have as educators?
2. What are some myths that our students may have about gratitude?
3. What are some activities we can try to help overcome or dispel the myths about gratitude?
4. At your school, can you set up "Gratitude Partners" or a "Gratitude Group" to help implement gratitude?

Chapter Five

Gratitude and Loss

Gratitude is our way of saying to all situations, "Welcome! I've been expecting you! Thank you for being here to help me learn and grow." We are always stronger, wiser, and filled more with peaceful power when we face each of life's lessons with this sort of grace.

—Doreen Virtue, PhD

GRATITUDE AND EMOTIONS

At this point, the question may be asked, "Do we always have to feel grateful?" Of course not. Gratitude should not be forced or faked. As stated earlier in this book, gratitude is much more than a pleasant emotion to be pondered occasionally. Gratitude should be an authentic way of living that motivates us and our students to positive action. Nevertheless, gratitude may be experienced in combination with other emotions and may, in fact, help us maintain some equilibrium in our lives and grow in resilience.

David Steindl-Rast, a monk who has written extensively about gratitude, says that we can't be grateful for everything. War, violence, or the loss of a loved one are things that we should not feel "grateful" for. On the other hand, he goes on to state that throughout these experiences, we can be grateful in every moment and learn and grow from all of life, even these painful experiences.

———————————————— ✕✕✕ ————————————————

Does Gratitude Mean No Sadness?

Once, a curious student asked, "If I am grateful all the time, then I won't have to be sad, right?" This made me think. What about some of the emotions that some people view as negative, like sadness, envy, pride, anger, shame, or fear? Well, I told the student that emotions are not positive or negative, they just exist and we should try to be aware of them and grow from them.

This sparked a great class discussion and here were some of the highlights. As humans, we have many different emotions to help us deal with life and all our experiences. We should never try to block emotions, but experience and process them. Then, I tried to give the students some imagery. If life was always sunny, our lives would turn into a desert. We need clouds and rain to keep things green and keep us growing.

Moreover, some emotions that may seem negative, like sadness, can actually help us. Sadness connects us to others who help us get through difficult situations. That sadness may also motivate us to reach out to a friend, family member, or trusted adult who can support us, which will make us feel closer to that person. Other emotions can also help keep us healthy: fear keeps us safe and anger can motivate us toward needed change in our lives.

How does gratitude relate to them? The class decided that no matter what emotion we are feeling, we can still choose to be grateful. For example, if we are feeling truly sad, this may be when we really need some gratitude to enable us to see the people who are helping us through a rough time.

RESEARCH ON GRATITUDE AND THINKING ABOUT DEATH

In a remarkable study called "Death and Gratitude: Death Reflection Enhances Gratitude," conducted by Eastern Washington University and Hofstra University, published in *The Journal of Positive Psychology* in March 2011, researchers showed that reflecting on death may actually help us become more grateful. This may seem counterintuitive, but the findings do put this entire subject in a new light. As stated in the study, "Becoming aware of one's mortal limitations enhances gratitude for the life that one has."

In the study, the participant's level of gratitude was measured and then each was placed in one of three groups. The first group was asked to visualize their usual daily routine. A second group was asked to articulate in writing their feelings and thoughts about death. The final group was asked to imagine something much more horrific; they were asked to visualize dying in a real-life scenario, "on the [twentieth] floor of an old, downtown building," after making "futile attempts to escape from the room and burning building before finally giving in to the fire and eventually death."

Upon completion of their mental exercise, all the groups were asked to record their level of gratitude. It is not surprising that the first group, where participants were asked to think about an average day, showed just a slight decrease in their level of reported gratitude. Subjects who recorded thoughts about death showed a small increase in their level of gratitude. However, with the final group, the results were astonishing. The gratitude levels climbed sharply with the group asked to visualize their deaths. In the study, the authors note that these dramatically rising levels of gratitude are similar to those who experience near-death experiences or a life-threatening illness.

Overall, our modern society does not deal with death very well. Anyone viewing advertising sees that we seem to worship youth and try to avoid any thought of death. This study shows that if we think about death and get a healthy perspective on it, we actually do become more grateful. Confronting this difficult subject may permit us to see every day and every moment of life as precious, as we grow in gratitude.

In the study, the authors note, "Reflecting on one's own death might help individuals take stock of this benefit and consequently increase their appreciation for life." Additionally, they wrote, "When one is pushed past their defenses of denying their own death, people tend to recognize 'what might not be' and become more grateful for the life they now experience. Fully recognizing one's own mortality may be an important aspect of the humble and grateful person."

HELPFUL BOOK

In an insightful book concerning this subject, *The Unwanted Gift of Grief*, Chaplain Timothy Van Duivendyck helps guide us through the painful process of grieving. Van Duivendyck says that when we express grief for someone who passed away, we are actually conveying gratitude for our loved one. This may seem strange, but those feelings of sadness, emptiness, and loneliness come from the love we felt and are expressions of gratitude. This idea helps us see how gratitude may be an aspect of the grieving process.

Losing My Brother Steve

One of the most challenging situations we may face in life is the loss of a loved one. I was fortunate that I had not lost anyone very close to me until a few years ago. This was when gratitude was truly put to the test, and I was able to see how gratitude can even help in the most challenging and painful parts of life. For me, this was when I lost my brother Steve.

In my life, one of the people I am most grateful for is my oldest brother, Steve. Steve was a musician, naturalist, and poet. He taught me how to play guitar, took me backpacking, encouraged me to read great literature, and inspired me to write. I am deeply grateful for all of these gifts he shared with me. I would not be writing this book without seeing his passion for writing.

Steve would describe the shamanistic power of words and how the act of writing had the power to heal us and also to articulate those aspects of life that seem impossible to pin down. He presented a new concept: that words have the power to create a bridge that connects the minds of the writer and reader and allows us to communicate even when space or time may separate us otherwise.

I feel that power of words more than ever because a few years ago, I lost my brother unexpectedly, but I still feel connected to him, especially as I read his writings. As I approach the anniversary of his passing, I have renewed gratitude for him. The gratitude for my brother grows and somewhat surprisingly, our relationship continues to grow.

When I started writing this book, I thanked him out loud. I smiled as I realized how vibrantly he is still with me. I know that physically losing someone does not end a relationship. As I see his influence in my life, I feel our relationship still grow.

The last time I was with Steve, we played guitar in our parents' backyard as the sun set. After replaying this scene in my head, I started to feel how gratitude could help my grieving by letting a little love and light come in to start the healing process. Every time I pick up a guitar, I am reminded of the gift of music he gave me. Now, I teach guitar and have the opportunity to give back a gift that Steve gave me. Every Friday, as I give my students a guitar concert or interject a song about the water cycle in a science lesson, Steve is with us.

After he passed away, I received my brother's Martin guitar. I had ambivalent feelings about getting it. I was afraid that having the guitar might remind me of how much I missed Steve. Thankfully, I didn't experience those negative feelings. When I opened the guitar case to find the smell of his cigarettes that I used to find unpleasant, the smell actually evoked a pleasant memory, reminding me of his presence and the times we played our guitars together.

Hesitantly, I shared this story with my students and brought Steve's guitar into the classroom to play for the students. I felt like this might be too painful to share or that it might bring up some sad memories. On the contrary, the students expressed gratitude for me sharing this part of my life with them. One student said it helped him feel a little better about his grandfather's recent death, that now he sees that the good memories can get him through the tough times. Another parent sent an email, saying that their daughter was so touched by the story of my brother, that she was finally able to talk about losing her grandmother and start the healing process.

I still have an ongoing conversation with Steve and feel his influence as well as his presence in my life. My son, who never met Steve, asks about him. I recount many stories of Steve and his intelligence, passion, and humor, as well as the gratitude I have for the gifts he gave that I can now pass on to others.

HELPING STUDENTS DEAL WITH LOSS

Helping students who are dealing with loss can be challenging. Always consult with school counselors and administrators when facing these situations. One way to begin the process of helping a student deal with loss may be as simple as listening compassionately, realizing that we have built up a relationship with the student and we may be able to offer support and stability throughout the grieving process.

Here are some other things to keep in mind when trying to help a student dealing with a loss:

- Contact school administrators, school counselors, and family members, when possible, to schedule a meeting to create a plan to help the student begin the healing process.
- Consider modifying the student's classwork, homework, and testing schedule for a set period of time.
- Keep in mind that students may grieve differently dependent on many factors, including their developmental stage.
- Prepare classmates so they will be sensitive and respond to the student in a positive manner, possibly making condolence cards, if that is appropriate.
- Remember that most of us are not trained counselors, so stay in close contact with the school counselors and administration as the situation progresses.

A helpful article, "Dealing with Death at School," from the National Association of School Psychologists, suggests these three areas to focus on to prepare educators to promote healing throughout the grieving process:

1. Prior planning
2. Empathetic leadership
3. Utilizing teachable moments

This article has valuable suggestions and useful resources for formulating a game plan and then gives the steps for successful implementation. A link to the article is listed in the appendix to this book.

Another valuable book is *The Grieving Student: A Teacher's Guide*, by Dr. David Schonfeld. This is an actual guidebook to help educators help students though the grieving process, described as the most "delicate issue" a teacher may ever encounter. But with the wisdom from this book, we may be a "lifeline" for the recovering student.

STEPPING STONES TO GRATITUDE

1. Sadness and the full range of emotions are part of life and gratitude can help us process them.
2. Losing someone close to us is extremely difficult but gratitude may help us.
3. Gratitude may help us through the hardest times in life and give us hope as we persist through these events.
4. As educators, we can help students through the grieving process with the help of school administrators and school counselors.

LET'S TALK ABOUT IT

1. Do we always have to feel grateful?
2. Should we "fake" gratitude?
3. How can gratitude help us deal with grief?
4. Does our school have a plan for dealing with students going through the grieving process or should we formulate a plan?

Chapter Six

Gratitude and Technology

Almost everything will work again if you unplug it for a few minutes . . . including you.

—Anne Lamott

Using technology seems to be a necessity in our modern lives. Yet even as technology gives us ways to make our lives easier and may help students to learn more efficiently, it also presents risks. As we navigate our digital world, simple guidelines and interjecting some gratitude will help keep us centered and grounded. This will also enable us to lead our students and children to a balanced life with regard to technology.

Every day, we see that technology has brought about many astonishing changes in our world, from lifesaving medical breakthroughs to more mundane, nevertheless just as transformative daily conveniences. The price of progress may be a digital world where people are missing out on actual life. It is sad, but also humorous to see people with their heads down, staring into their smartphones, walking like zombies, and missing everything going on around them.

In addition, obesity has been linked with the sedentary habits of watching television or utilizing media time in children and adolescents, according to *Pediatrics*, the official journal of American Academy of Pediatrics. The alarming rise of obesity is something that should make us all take pause and think about ways we can encourage healthy habits in ours students.

Interestingly, one irony in the advancement of technology is that what was purported to allow us to work less and to enjoy life more has resulted in many of us actually working more. Now that we are able to connect to the office virtually anywhere, it is challenging to have time to ourselves or family time that is protected from distractions. However, with some healthy guidelines, we can enjoy technology's benefits while avoiding the dangers.

DIGITAL DISTRACTIONS

Today, many of us face the challenge of limiting our screen time. It is almost like we hear our technology devices calling us, tempting us to disengage from whatever we are doing in real life and check email or Facebook. Sometimes, we do have a legitimate reason to do this, like a sick child or a situation at work that must be handled from long distance, but much of the time that we are on our smartphones is not necessary and can wait.

Sometimes, it seems people are more interested in posting where they are on Facebook instead of just enjoying being there. Out at dinner in a nice restaurant, some people will be looking at their latest high tech device instead of engaging the people they are with or soaking up the ambiance. Amusingly, a friend tells her husband, "We are spending too much money to be eating out at this restaurant, so please put away your phone and try to enjoy it."

Dad at the Park

At the park one day, I watched as a boy joyously yelled to his dad, "Look, Dad, I finally made it up the climbing wall!" His dad had his head down looking at his phone and said, "Yeah, I see you." The boy stopped and had a look of sadness and disappointment descend across his face. It appeared that this wasn't the first time this had happened. At that point, I made a promise to myself that I wouldn't turn into that dad, missing the best parts of my son's life.

Thus far, I have done okay, but finding time to write this book has been challenging. It is summer right now, and I take time to write every morning. Then I spend the rest of the day with my family. However, I find thoughts coming to me that I feel I must get down before I forget, so I rush to the computer to record them. My son looked at me one day as I interrupted a family activity and said quietly, "Dad, I hate your computer." Since then, I have left my computer off during family time. Those ideas for the book can wait, but my family can't.

Recently, a colleague changed jobs to have more time with his family, but took a cut in salary. With the new job, he does not have to keep his company phone on or respond to work situations from home. He said, "We can make more money, but we can't make more time and I am thankful that I can have more priceless time with my family."

TECHNOLOGY RESEARCH

If adults have almost constant technological diversions, how does this impact our students? They have all the distractions that we have as adults, perhaps more with today's technology, where everything is instantaneously at their fingertips and they are connected to their friends continuously.

In some ways, teenagers and college students face even greater challenges when it comes to digital distractions. A compelling study from August 2014, conducted at Baylor University and published in the *Journal of Behavioral Addictions*, tracked cell phone use by college students. What they found was alarming:

- Female college students spent an average of ten hours a day on their cell phones.
- Male college students spent an average of eight hours a day on their cell phones.

Furthermore, the study noted that an estimated 60 percent of the participants in the study were "addicted" to their cell phones. Dr. James Roberts, one of the authors of the study, said that those students admitted that they get anxious when the cell phone is not in sight and that they can't live without it. Addiction may be a little too strong a word here, but the point is well made. Finally, the study noted that cell phone use exhibits the paradox of modern technology—that it can be "freeing and enslaving at the same time."

HEALTHY TECHNOLOGY GUIDELINES

What are some of the solutions to these findings? According to *Psychology Today*, here are guidelines to help us model a balanced approach to technology for our students and children:

- Ensure there are daily times when we turn off all electronic devices and talk to another human being face-to-face.
- Find balance between screen time and in-person time each week. For every hour we invest in front of a screen, invest the same amount of time with stimulating human contact.
- Experiment with a technology "fast" every month, where we actually go for a day or more without any technological devices. Later in this chapter, we will explore what to do with that new free time.
- Avoid disruptions of our sleep by placing the phone at least fifteen feet away from the bed when we sleep or simply buy an alarm clock and turn off the cell phone.

- Every day, try to have time for family and friends, uninterrupted by technology. Also, enjoy the simple pleasures of life, like getting out in nature or reading a book, not on a Kindle, but a real book. Feel the joy and peace this brings.
- Find a few minutes to experience peaceful solitude.

TECHNOLOGY FAST

Taking the idea of a technology "fast" to our fourth-grade classroom, we did an exercise pertaining to electronics and gratitude. We asked the students to give up screen time for a whole weekend, meaning they would not get on a smartphone, computer, watch TV, or play any video games. This was a voluntary activity. We did not know how many students would be brave enough to try this.

Out of twenty-seven students in the class, fifteen volunteered for this challenge. We did pledge a modest reward of a class coupon to redeem at the treasure box if they made it through the technology fast and filled some of that time with their choice of a gratitude activity.

Out of the fifteen students who volunteered to try this extreme challenge, only five made it. This actually seems like it was an encouraging outcome. We asked them to do something extreme and five of them succeeded. Each of the five students volunteered stories of how difficult it was, but they also reveled in the rewards they gained.

Ana

One girl who succeeded in this experiment was named Ana. She said that she talked about this challenge with her whole family and they all tried it. It was a spring weekend and her family spent most of the time outdoors. She even took some of the time outdoors to work on her gratitude journal and make a gratitude drawing, depicting her family having a picnic. Joyfully, they played hide and seek. Ana said that after this weekend, her family now tries to limit screen time on the weekends and make it outdoors more often.

A MORE MODERATE CHALLENGE

After the extreme challenge of the technology fast, we modified it, asking the students to include their families and agree on a weekend where they would "limit" their screen time to an agreed upon amount and fill the extra time with family or gratitude activities. Almost all the students in the class agreed to partake in this adventure. We still had a few holdouts and that was okay. Out of the twenty-seven students, twenty-four volunteered to try it and nineteen successfully completed a version of limiting their screen time.

The following Monday, students triumphantly recounted how they enjoyed reconnecting with their family members and friends. Everyone who tried it delighted in the break from the routine. One boy humorously said that he almost gave his parents a heart attack when he volunteered to clean up after the dog in the backyard with the new time he had to fill. Another student gleefully talked about playing outside all day long, enjoying the sunshine and the new spring flowers in her backyard.

An additional student said she was grateful that she had a chance to teach a sibling how to play chess. Putting on a family talent show was a creative way for a different student to enjoy his time away from technology. Also, two students and their families got together and had a picnic on a mountain. On the picnic, the students led the adults in a quick verbal gratitude list. A final student said simply that she never realized how much she would enjoy reading outside under a tree.

One family started a game night that they still enjoy weekly. Hiking was the physical outlet that another family discovered, finding some beautiful trails five miles from their house that they never knew existed. All these activities were gladly recorded on the students' gratitude logs on Monday morning.

After hearing other students happily share their experiences, one of the students who did not volunteer for this activity and who originally said that limiting screen time would be impossible actually said he would try it. The following week, he came back and said it was hard to get away from a new video game, but he loved going to a trampoline playground with his family and a friend. All these activities came to fruition as time opened up that had been monopolized by technology. What started as a sacrifice for many of the students transformed into a joy.

My Family's Screen Time Solution

One morning, I woke up bleary eyed with my jubilant six-year-old son asking for breakfast. As I prepared his favorite cinnamon cheese toast with a side of fresh strawberries and blueberries, he asked, "Can I watch Kid's PBS while you make breakfast?" I said okay and proceeded to make the meal.

My wife woke and saw what was happening and said, "Why is our son watching TV? Don't you remember that we said no screen time before breakfast?" I told her that I didn't remember that. The TV got turned off and my son was upset. We all had an uncomfortably quiet breakfast and then I had to leave for an appointment. As I was driving, I was brainstorming for a solution to the problem and I came up with a few options.

But when I called my wife to check in, she said that she had asked our son to help her construct "Screen Time Guidelines" we would all live by. Here is what they came up with:

1. *Weekday/school day = 1 hour screen time (time it!)*
2. *Weekends = 2 hours screen time per day*
3. *No screen time during meals or homework (Must finish meals and homework before screen time. Homework first!)*
4. *No screen time before breakfast*
5. *No violent video games*
6. *Chores can be done to earn extra screen time (vacuum, dust, make bed, etc.)*
7. *No video games and TV at the same time*

At the bottom of the guidelines, my son drew a picture of all of us (as stick figures of course) converging on one heart, all appearing to be connected to that heart with love.

I was truly overwhelmed with the list they assembled and the picture my son drew. Now, when faced with a family dilemma, we use this method of working together to try to come to a common solution when possible. With the guidelines in place, breakfast went back to being the pleasure it should be, with my son even reciting a gratitude or two.

FOUR MORE TIPS FOR USING MEDIA WISELY

The Center on Media and Child Health has a superb website at http://cmch. tv/parents, with a database of research and many tools for parents and teachers. On the website they list four tips for helping our students and children use media wisely:

1. Utilize media mindfully.
2. Watch for problematic behavior.
3. Be a media role model.
4. Remove screens from children's bedrooms.

POSITIVE USES OF TECHNOLOGY

With these guidelines set in place, technology does present some truly remarkable opportunities for educators and students. Technology opens up opportunities for twenty-first century skills, such as the four Cs:

1. Critical thinking
2. Communication
3. Collaboration
4. Creativity

These twenty-first century skills prepare students for life and the rapidly changing technological world. Furthermore, students may conduct research with the use of technology and participate in long-distance learning. Playing educational computer games may help students learn a wide range of subjects from math facts to anatomy in an engaging fashion, keeping their attention and adjusting the lesson to accommodate their learning level and the speed of mastering the knowledge. This is an area that holds seemingly unlimited promise. Integrated with a balanced approach to education, technology will help us educate and prepare our students for their futures.

TECHNOLOGY AND GRATITUDE

How can gratitude help us balance our use of technology? First of all, we need to realize that gratitude is its own kind of technology. Unplugging from technology periodically allows us time to reflect and become truly grateful. When we take even a few minutes away from digital distractions to focus on gratitude, we are recalibrating ourselves and becoming grounded again. This is even more imperative when life gets hectic and our stress levels rise.

One gratitude activity to try is to set a timer for just one minute. We can close our eyes, if we can't get away from our computer, take a deep breath and think of whom we are really grateful for right now and why they are important to us, as well as the things they do for us. Taking just this one minute and delving deeply into gratitude can refresh us and restore some sanity to our frantic day.

Like the students demonstrated earlier in this chapter, some of our screen time may be replaced with a gratitude activity. Could we also integrate a gratitude activity with screen time? Sure, we can even write someone a quick email, telling them how grateful we are for them. Gratitude lists on the computer are wonderful ways to count our blessings. Personally, I still keep a gratitude list I started over ten years ago on my computer and enjoy going back and reading over the things I have been grateful for at different times in my life.

Lastly, we can think of the positive ways technology impacts our lives, such as making many aspects of our lives easier and more efficient. This can help us temper our frustration when a technological device is not working as quickly as we would like or if our computer suddenly crashes on us. Instead of throwing the device out the window, as many of us feel like doing sometimes, we can take a breath and remember that technology is something to be grateful for.

─────────────────────────❈─────────────────────────

Technology and the First Date

Here is an example of how technology is impacting some teens' lives. A good friend and colleague who teaches at a local high school told me an intriguing story. One night, she was out at a restaurant and saw two girls she recognized as her students across the room. Looking closer, it appeared that these two girls were out on a double date with two boys. The funny part was that no one was talking or even looking at each other; they were all texting on their cell phones.

My friend didn't think much of it, but followed up with the girls the next time she saw them at school. She asked the girls if they were on a date, and they replied that yes, they were on a first date with these two boys. Puzzled, my colleague inquired, "Then why were you on your phones texting the whole time?" One of the girls replied, "We had to text each other to see how the date was going."

Ironically, the girls were texting to see how the date was going instead of actually being on the date. My friend ended the conversation on a funny note, saying "When I was dating, we had to go to the bathroom together to check how things were going, but at least we were talking to our dates throughout the night."

─────────────────────────❈─────────────────────────

STEPPING STONES TO GRATITUDE

1. Technology is part of our modern lives, giving us medical breakthroughs and daily conveniences, yet also presents challenges to a balanced life.
2. Technology may be a distraction and make it more difficult to be "present" in our lives.
3. Simple guidelines help us encourage student's balanced use of technology.
4. Limiting screen time helps students and adults lead a more balanced life.
5. Technology can help students prepare for our rapidly changing world.
6. Gratitude may be interjected into our technological lives, helping us stay grounded.

LET'S TALK ABOUT IT

1. Does technology get in the way of living a balanced life?
2. What are some strategies for using technology wisely as a family and individually?
3. What are some positive uses of technology for our students?

Part II

APPLYING GRATITUDE

Chapter Seven

Giving Students the Gift of Gratitude

We can only be said to be alive in those moments when our hearts are conscious of our treasures.

—Thornton Wilder

Of all the character strengths we can teach our students, gratitude is one of the most powerful and malleable. Gratitude contributes to our happiness and helps create meaning in our work and lives. Fueling our teaching, gratitude can propel us into a positive flow in the classroom, engaging our students and sparking our passion about education. In addition, gratitude is contagious— when we practice it, we can't help but spread it around to our students, colleagues, and everyone we come in contact with, starting a mini-revolution in our world. But gratitude does require some work and conscious focus that we will learn in this chapter.

MAKING A CHANGE WITH GRATITUDE

Remarkably, the average adult has over sixty thousand separate thoughts on a daily basis, according to the National Science Foundation. More interesting, these may be the same thoughts as yesterday and tomorrow. Thus, many of us trudge through life thinking similar thoughts every day. Now, if we are satisfied with our lives, this is acceptable. However, if we want to change our lives and our classrooms, we need to make room for some change. Gratitude can help change some of those thoughts and lead to changing our lives, and in turn, the lives of our students.

HOW TO TRANSFORM OUR CLASSROOMS
WITH CONSCIOUS GRATITUDE

Before introducing the practice of gratitude to our students, we should try creating our own gratitude lists or another gratitude activity to experience the process ourselves. Then, we will be able to model it more easily, persuasively, and powerfully. We can also share how practicing gratitude changed our feelings and behavior.

As teachers and as parents, we know that we can teach, most effectively, behavior that we practice. As the saying goes, "Your actions speak so loud, I can't hear what you're saying." As we grow stronger with an attitude of gratitude and display it in our lives, it will be easier to share this virtue with our students and colleagues.

Interestingly, gratitude seems to work like a muscle and the physical action of writing a gratitude list helps develop "gratitude muscles." As stated in the last chapter, for those of us who are comfortable with technology, we may find that keeping a gratitude journal on our smartphones or our computers can be equally powerful and easier to keep current.

Practicing conscious gratitude gives us an opportunity to choose our attitude every day. The gratitude practice is more likely to take off in our classrooms as we become passionate about it. Subsequently, many students may become passionate about gratitude, reminding each other to choose their attitudes and truly make every day a great day. Before long, we may find that parents also notice the changes in their children and adopt gratitude into their lives, spreading the positive message.

THE RESEARCH AND REWARDS OF GRATITUDE

After a couple of weeks of implementing gratitude, we may then introduce the body of gratitude research to the students and their parents. This research supports the effectiveness of gratitude in the classroom. The scientific studies demonstrate the power of gratitude to help students and adults in numerous areas. This is extremely exciting as we watch this field of study grow and develop. We can all find hope here.

Recent compelling research by two leaders in the field of gratitude and education, Dr. Robert Emmons from the University of California, Davis, and Dr. Jeffrey Froh from Hofstra University, strongly supports the idea that gratitude helps students and adults. The research illustrates how keeping a gratitude journal on a daily basis helps students achieve the following:

• Higher grades and higher goals
• More satisfaction with relationships, life, and school

- Less materialism
- More helpful, generous, and compassionate behavior
- More resilience when stressed
- More joy and pleasure
- Feel less lonely and isolated

For adults, keeping a gratitude journal enables people to:

- Be more optimistic and happy
- Experience more social satisfaction and be more outgoing
- Exercise more often
- Cultivate a stronger immune system
- Feel more forgiving
- Experience more joy and pleasure
- Have less envy and depression
- Have fewer physical complaints and sleep better.

The Gratitude Conference

Recently, I attended a "Transforming our Classrooms with Gratitude Conference" at the Greater Good Center for Science at University of California, Berkeley. This conference was truly astonishing in the way it showed the power and actual practicality of utilizing gratitude in the classroom. Twenty-five experts in social-emotional learning, along with twenty-five teachers explored the latest curriculum that is being tested throughout the country through the Youth Gratitude Project, generously funded by the John Templeton Foundation.

During the conference, we saw the latest gratitude research, presented by Dr. Giacomo Bono, a leader of this project. I was able to give a brief presentation about my experience with gratitude in the classroom and then participate in focus groups, as we worked to create new gratitude activities that could seamlessly work in our classrooms. The ones that seemed most easily applicable were the activities that aligned with current classroom exercises, like making writing a gratitude letter part of an English lesson or studying a historical figures use of gratitude in achieving their goals and helping humanity.

The use of gratitude in the classroom is expanding rapidly, and the resources we will be able to share and utilize effectively will grow quickly. This is encouraging news to all of us who are trying to refine and improve our implementation of gratitude in our lives and in our classrooms. Most importantly, as we are helping our students practice gratitude, we are reshaping the world.

THE GRATITUDE JOURNAL

As mentioned earlier, it is ideal if we begin the gratitude journal at the beginning of the school year, listing five gratitudes every day. By the end of the year, we will each have a thousand gratitudes. Research has also shown that it may be more important to delve deeper into each individual gratitude, rather than focusing on the number of gratitudes per day. Thus, we can ask our students to record fewer gratitudes and instead dig deeper by writing the second part of the gratitude, using "because" in the prompt. This template is an example:

1. Thank you for _____
   because_____
2. Thank you for _____
   because_____
3. Thank you for _____
   because_____

Try writing a short list on the board to help our students begin. Tell them they can "borrow" a gratitude from our list if they are having trouble starting. A few examples include being thankful for:

- Feeling the abundance of love in our lives
- Being healthy
- Having friends, both old and new
- Being alive
- Having food to eat and clothes to wear

With all gratitude activities, we can suggest that the students be as specific as possible and look at the costs and benefits underlying the gratitude, as Dr. Froh mentioned in the foreword of this book. For example, instead of writing "Thank you for lunch," they can write, "Thank you for the tomatoes and lettuce in my salad and all the people who made it possible, from the farmer, to the truck driver, the store clerk, and my parents who had to work and spend some money to buy it," or "Thank you for the nutritious lunch made by loving hands and the time and effort it took them because food strengthens our bodies and love nourishes our soul."

We can even write, "Thank you for all the bad stuff that happens to me because it helps me grow in new ways." We can be grateful for things that seem to be bad at the time, seeing the lessons we learn and new opportunities that come from them. These are lessons in courage, wisdom, persistence, and fortitude. If we want to really challenge our students, ask if they can be thankful for homework or chores. This challenge enables the students to see what is good about homework (it helps them learn and prepares them for life).

WHAT DO WE CONTROL?

To explore the importance of gratitude as it relates to our lives, ask students, "Are there things in life that we do not control?" Creative students come up with answers beyond the weather and the behavior of others. Stop the list after generating twenty-five items or so. Then ask, "What do we have control over?" This is a little harder for some, but eventually they all get it—the only thing we can control is ourselves.

More specifically, we control our actions, our attitude, and our awareness. These exercises in gratitude will help us with all three areas. When we are grateful for everything given to us in life, we will have a positive attitude and our actions will also be more positive. When we focus on the positive, our awareness of the positive grows. Gratitude is more than a feeling, it is a choice. By practicing it consistently, we make this choice a fundamental attitude that guides our lives in and out of the classroom.

Furthermore, remind the students that their gratitudes should be authentic, but they don't need to be overwhelming. If students get stuck, ask them to think about what they get to do today and include that on their list. The important word in that last sentence is "get." When we are authentically grateful, we "get" to do things instead of "having" to do them. For example, many people hate waiting in line. In our fast-paced, technological society, with everything at our fingertips, many of us are impatient with even a one-minute wait. But now, we can think of this opportunity as "getting" to wait in line and take that time to make a quick gratitude list.

THE BENEFITS OF GRATITUDE

Once a week, it is beneficial to go around the class and share our favorite gratitudes. We will most likely be encouraged and pleasantly surprised by what our students share. We will learn about things going on in their lives that we might not hear about otherwise. This will help build a positive culture in our classrooms. Interestingly, we might see the benefits of gratitude from students and also from their parents. Parents report that their children are less selfish and more willing to help their families after doing gratitude exercises.

GRATITUDE IN ACTION

Astonishingly, after we practiced the gratitude list for about a month, one student asked if we could start a "Gratitude in Action" list. He said that if we were really grateful, we should show it by helping others. The class discussion that ensued was truly remarkable. One student said that they heard that love was a verb, an action, and maybe that was true with gratitude also. We all agreed emphatically. This was one of those powerful moments that impacts everyone in the classroom, facilitated by grateful students.

The "Gratitude in Action" list became something they looked forward to sharing every day. Students began to voluntarily help fellow students, family, and neighbors. Increasingly, they became more active in their churches, groups, and clubs, or joined new ones. These students demonstrated that gratitude is more than a pleasant feeling for them—it may become a way of consciously living and taking action in our world to make it better.

The Challenge: Taking the Action of Gratitude to the Next Level

When my students started talking about "Gratitude in Action," I told them about a friend who says that every day she tries to do a good deed and not get "found out." This could be paying for someone's toll or even something more mundane, like vacuuming the house and not telling anyone.

This friend tells an inspiring story about how this started. She was given the task of doing a good act and not taking any credit. She couldn't think of anything to do, so she was assigned (by another friend) to take a bouquet of flowers into a local nursing home, tell the receptionist to give it to a patient who never gets any visitors, and quietly walk out before the receptionist can thank her or ask any questions.

After some resistance, she did it and made a clean getaway, saying the receptionist looked pleasantly puzzled. Feeling elated, she immediately took out her cell phone to call her friend and tell her the story. Luckily, she caught herself before she made the call and put the cell phone away. For two days, she was bursting with this news and could hardly contain herself from sharing it.

This is where the exercise took on an unexpected dimension. She realized that when we tell others about the "good deeds" we do, we are getting the reward right there. But by keeping it anonymous and not telling anyone, we are cultivating a feeling inside ourselves that she described as "a ray of sunshine inside our hearts" that kept growing and growing.

When we first started talking about showing our gratitude in action and not getting caught, the students came up with some creative actions to take, like:

• *Mowing a neighbor's lawn*

- *Cleaning up trash at a local park*
- *Cleaning up their room or a messy sibling's room*
- *Giving cash stealthily to a church at offering time*
- *Being quiet when they feel like yelling at a sibling*
- *Setting the table while no one is looking*
- *Eating "yucky" vegetables with a smile*
- *Babysitting younger siblings without complaining*

But this is where gratitude takes on an entirely new dimension. During our class discussion, a truly thoughtful student commented that my friend should have gone back to the nursing home and asked to talk to the recipient of the flowers, letting them know why the flowers were left for them. The student said that if someone really wanted to help a lonely person in a nursing home, they should visit them once a week and get to know them. This would not violate the challenge because they wouldn't have to tell anyone else about it.

Impressed with the idea, the students asked if we could try this as a class. We actually found an organization that helps match students with seniors who need companionship. Currently, we are moving forward to implement this idea, thanks to a thoughtful student taking this story in a new and powerful direction.

Finally, the students said they would give everyone in our classroom and all their families a challenge or experiment for the week: for all of us to find a good deed to do and not to get caught or tell anyone and see if we feel that light that will grow inside us. Then, repeat the challenge often. They asked if we could try this with everyone at our school. That is our next challenge, as we try to reshape our school and the world with the altruistic actions of gratitude.

SUPPLEMENTING OUR GRATITUDE WORKOUT

As stated before, gratitude works like a muscle. It will atrophy if not cultivated. We also need to alter the workout periodically to keep the muscles growing and balanced. As we see in the classroom constantly, one size doesn't need to fit all; just as not all students respond to lessons in the same manner, gratitude should be presented with options.

To avoid gratitude fatigue and burnout, try new activities with your students. Other activities may include sending home a gratitude album, which students and their families may decorate any way they want. In class, display and celebrate the wonderful artwork and gratitude activities the students enjoy with their families. Give them a week to create a page for your classroom gratitude album that will last the entire school year and beyond.

Another idea to prevent gratitude burnout is to find the students' strengths and then use those strengths to express gratitude. Many students know their strengths or we may have recognized them already. If we are having trouble identifying strengths, we can use an instrument like a "Character Inventory" from the Internet. Check the appendix for the VIA Character Inventory website.

One colleague offered a story of a student who wanted to express his gratitude to a fellow teacher. He asked if he could draw a picture, as drawing was one of his strengths. When he presented the drawing of himself giving a beautiful bouquet of flowers to the other teacher, they were all moved to tears.

Later in this book, we will examine a variety of other gratitude activities and exercises that have been shown to be effective.

STEPPING STONES TO GRATITUDE

1. Gratitude is a teaching tool that can transform our classrooms and lives.
2. A decade's worth of research shows that gratitude is effective in increasing students' achievement and engagement.
3. Gratitude journals are a powerful way to start the process.
4. The benefits of gratitude are seen in the lives of our students and their families.
5. Gratitude may enable teachers to do their jobs more effectively.
6. Other gratitude exercises supplement the gratitude journal in the classroom to help students' continual growth.

LET'S TALK ABOUT IT

1. What does the research say about the benefits of gratitude?
2. How can we introduce gratitude in our classrooms?
3. What are some ways we can successfully begin gratitude journals with our students?
4. Of all the activities presented in this chapter, what do you think would work best with you, your students, and your colleagues?

Chapter Eight

Mindfulness and Gratitude

All of humanity's problems stem from man's inability to sit quietly in a room alone.

—Blaise Pascal

INTRODUCTION TO MINDFULNESS

Wherever we are and whatever we are doing, life is always experienced in the present moment, unfolding before us. However, we spend much of our time worrying about the future or regretting the past. Being mindful is a way to train our minds to be more present in life and also in our classrooms.

When we practice mindfulness and gratitude together, making it a habit, life is not so stressful and we become more effective and efficient, learning to enjoy life in its full range of actions and emotions. Mindfulness does not need to be connected to any religion. By itself, it is a potent tool that can make the difference between truly living and merely existing.

To some teachers, mindfulness may not seem applicable in our classrooms. It might seem to be a more esoteric practice, left to people who want to explore alternative spiritual practices. However, recent research has shown that mindfulness is a powerful tool in the classroom with new applications being discovered constantly. Any teacher may learn this simple skill with a little practice and even share it with his or her students.

The Story of Desta

One of the kindest and most energetic students I ever had the pleasure of teaching was a girl named Desta. She surprised me constantly, mostly in a positive way. She was a deep thinker and extremely friendly with a hidden source of seemingly boundless energy. We could all tell that she would always be the life of the party.

However, sometimes Desta was fidgety and on occasion had trouble focusing. After our class started a simple mindfulness exercise of being silent for a short time, Desta told me that it was helping her tremendously. She said that before we started doing this, she was uncomfortable sitting still and at times found it hard to slow down her racing mind. At first, she dreaded the time when we would take our deep breaths and sit quietly.

But slowly, she got comfortable, and now, throughout the day, she does our "exercise" and composes a gratitude list in that silence. Gratitude combined with mindfulness seemed to be the missing piece for her. Now, she said she had something positive to fill the uncomfortable silence. At night, when going to sleep is challenging, she takes some deep breaths and reflects on all the good things that happened that day before she peacefully drifts off to sleep.

Moreover, she said that practicing mindfulness helped her focus in school and actually do better in math, always a challenging subject for her. Along with many other students, Desta exemplifies how combining mindfulness with grati-tude may help students find balance in their lives, as well as learning to focus more effectively, allowing them to achieve academically.

WHAT IS MINDFULNESS?

To begin this discussion, what is mindfulness? Another word for mindfulness is focus, like focusing a laser beam on a target. Mindfulness is simply focus-ing our attention on the present moment, fully engaged in whatever activity we are doing. Another way to look at the idea of focusing our attention is to realize that the same amount of gunpowder is in a firecracker as in a bullet. The bullet is so much more powerful because all that energy is focused in one direction. Likewise, when we focus our attention through the use of mindful-ness, we become much more effective.

CHALLENGES TO MINDFULNESS

Once, a friend asked an interesting question about mindfulness, "If we are totally focused on the present, don't we miss out on learning from the past or planning for the future?" Practicing mindfulness does not mean that we do not learn from the past or plan for the future. It simply means that we try to stay focused on whatever activity we are doing. For many of us, we are far too distracted throughout the day, trying to do many things at once and not doing any of them efficiently.

In our lives, it seems we have two general modes. One is where we are mindful, aware and present in the moment. The other mode is being on "automatic pilot," not fully aware. Depending on many factors, such as how physically and mentally tired we are, we may bounce between the two states, but many of us get stuck in automatic mode.

If we are in automatic mode, we do not have the opportunity to learn, to grow, or to connect with others. This is a challenge for everyone, but as educators, this is even more hazardous because a teacher on automatic pilot misses many opportunities to help students. At times, we seem to be hypnotized by the monologue going on in our heads, losing the potential magic of the moment. Becoming more mindful helps guide us back into the present.

RESEARCH: MINDFULNESS AND STUDENTS

We have looked at what mindfulness is and some challenges to mindfulness. Now, let's look at some research. In a recent study from the *Journal of Applied Developmental Psychology*, fourth- and fifth-grade students who practiced mindfulness exercises improved their math scores by 15 percent. Another remarkable finding from this study demonstrated that students as young as nine exhibited the positive effects. In addition, other areas of the student's life were affected, including dramatically improved positive outlook, less aggressive behavior, and improved social skills.

Compared to the control group, the students who took part in the mindfulness training showed the following:

- 82 percent had a more positive outlook
- 81 percent learned to make themselves happy
- 58 percent tried to help others more often
- 24 percent more social behavior
- 24 percent less aggressive behavior
- 20 percent increase in being perceived as pro-social
- 15 percent higher math scores
- Higher cognitive control, emotional control, empathy, and optimism

Now that we have looked at the effect of mindfulness on students, let's turn to what mindfulness can do for teachers.

MINDFULNESS FOR TEACHERS

In a recent study from the University of Wisconsin's Center for the Investigation of the Mind, Lisa Flock conducted an eight-week pilot study to train teachers to be more mindful in the classroom, helping them be more patient and focused. As teachers, we know this can be extremely challenging, because we are asked to attend to many tasks at once.

In the study, teachers who completed the training experienced less stress and burnout in addition to becoming more effective teachers. In the classroom, mindfulness can also help refocus our attention to teach properly when we are becoming frustrated for any reason, giving us a chance to save a challenging lesson. When we stumble as we deliver the lesson, we can simply take a deep breath and refocus.

In writing about this study in the Greater Good Science Center at the University of California, Berkeley, Vickie Zakrzewski says, "The study suggests that when teachers practice mindfulness, students' misbehavior and other stressors become like water off a duck's back, allowing them to stay focused on what teachers really want to do: teach." In addition, this study also reminds us that mindfulness does not happen overnight. Like exercise, it must be done consistently to reap the benefits and those benefits do pay off generously.

A USEFUL BOOK: *THE MIRACLE OF MINDFULNESS*

One book that makes mindfulness much easier to understand *is The Miracle of Mindfulness: An Introduction to the Practice of Meditation,* by Thich Nhat Hanh. This book says that most people are too busy to be mindful. In the classroom, things may become so hectic that we forget to think of mindfulness. Teachers, like so many others, think that they have too much to do, too many loose ends to tie up, and not enough time to be mindful. Hanh poses an appropriate question, "What is the value of an activity if it is done with impatience or anger?"

Furthermore, Hanh goes on to affirm that mindfulness allows us to feel the peace that flows to us when we do one small step at a time and are fully engaged in what we are doing. As teachers, many will recount profoundly enjoyable moments when everyone in the classroom is on the same page and fully engaged in whatever activity is taking place. We may have been mindful without even realizing it. When it comes down to it, mindfulness is the goal in the classroom for everyone, teachers and students.

What are the penalties for not being mindful? According to Hanh, when we are not mindful, our energy is dispersed, almost like confetti, and we become forgetful. Life seems like a struggle. How many of us have felt like that in the classroom? To be mindful is to have new energy and live in the moment.

To exemplify these ideas about mindfulness, Hanh refers to another author, the celebrated Russian writer Leo Tolstoy, who expressed mindfulness beautifully when he wrote a short story about the three most important questions is life:

1. When is the best time to do something?
2. Who are the most important people to listen to?
3. What is the most important thing to do?

In the story, the answers to the questions were:

1. The right time to do something is now.
2. The people to listen to are the ones with you now.
3. The most important thing to do is to make those people happy.

In our classroom and lives, if we ask these questions and remind ourselves of the answers, our classrooms and our lives will be happier and more effective.

METHODS TO BEING MINDFUL

As teachers, mindfulness is a valuable tool, yet it still may be difficult to practice in the midst of our extremely busy days. Throughout the book, Hanh gives some simple methods to help us begin to become more mindful. Moreover, he says that we often "forget" to be mindful, so we should establish some simple habits that will become routine to help us become more mindful.

BREATHING

The first habit is to focus on breathing. Hanh says, "To master our breath is to be in control of our bodies and our minds." Of course, we all breathe every second of every day, but breathing mindfully gives it a new power and depth. Here, it is helpful to remember the story of the fish, when asked how the water felt, the fish said, "What is water?" Often, we forget that the way we breathe has a profound effect on our mindfulness and physiology.

When we are upset, worried, or simply stressed out, we tend to breathe more shallowly and not get the oxygen deep in our lungs, where it needs to go. If we can stop in the midst of our busy days and take a deep breath or two, returning our awareness to the present moment, it helps put things in perspective. Simple yet powerful habits, like taking a deep breath every time we get in our car or stop at a red light, may become healthy habits that remind us to stay mindful no matter how chaotic our day becomes.

It is helpful to start the day by taking some deep and cleansing breaths, before we feel the pressure of the day begin as we start our morning rituals, maybe even breathing deeply as we say our morning prayers, if that is the routine. In addition, we can give ourselves other prompts, like taking a deep breath before we check our email or even when our coffee or tea is brewing in the morning.

A friend suggests an effective technique to try to implement this in our lives: when agitated or upset, simply count your breaths backwards from nine to one. Counting backwards as we breathe forces us to focus on the numbers. Each time we take a breath, go a little deeper and slowly feel some peace returning. Trying this in stressful situations, like a tense parent meeting, helps keep us calm and mindful, where we would have felt mounting levels of strain. The result of employing this technique may be that we think up a creative solution to problems that would have eluded our anxious minds.

THE HALF-SMILE

Of all the methods presented in Hanh's book, one of the most interesting is the idea that we can keep a "half-smile" throughout the day no matter what happens. Hanh says that keeping a half-smile helps us stay in the moment and not lose ourselves in the stress of the day. This idea of the half-smile corresponds strongly with gratitude. If we are practicing gratitude in our lives, that half-smile is easy to cultivate and display. In fact, that half-smile can become a whole smile.

A DAY OF MINDFULNESS

Finally, the last habit presented in the book is the idea of taking a day to become more mindful. Hanh suggests that we take one day out of the week to become more mindful. We may take extra time doing the dishes or even grading papers, but doing it mindfully, keeping our attention focused on the task, doing it slowly and purposefully will help instill this new and powerful habit.

In our hectic lives, even if we don't have an entire day to be mindful, we can take an hour and focus on the people around us and the activity we are doing. Like anything, the more we do it, the easier it becomes. If we do find our mind wandering, we gently bring it back to the present moment.

Mindfulness Ideas for Life

Taking just a few quiet minutes to start our day may help transform our lives and our classrooms. Personally, I set my alarm for ten minutes before I need to get up, so I can spend that time in quiet contemplation even before I get ready for my day. Then, it radically alters the day and I do not miss the ten minutes of sleep because I am setting up my day so I can be at peace, no matter what happens.

This quiet time helps me slow down and sets a peaceful foundation. Also, on the way home from work, I sometimes stop for five minutes and sit quietly under a huge oak tree. This clears out any garbage from the day and allows me to be with my family and give them 100 percent, being completely present without carrying any stress home from work.

MINDFULNESS AND GRATITUDE

One thing we can all do to become more mindful is to bring more silence into our lives, integrating it into daily routine. David Steindl-Rast, a Catholic monk who writes extensively about gratitude, says we need to stop in order to be grateful. He even goes so far to say we need to build "stop signs" into our lives to practice mindfulness and gratitude.

Mindfulness can be a "launching pad" for gratitude, helping us slow down, reflect, and build awareness of all we have to be thankful for. Gratitude and mindfulness are inextricably intertwined because we become more grateful as we see the world around us more clearly. We see the world as it is with gratitude and mindfulness, not as we think it should be.

Silence in the Classroom (A New Kind of Silence)

When I started teaching, I asked my new principal if she had any activities she would recommend to implement in my classroom. Immediately, she replied, "Help your students get comfortable with silence by taking some quiet time in your class every day." I was intrigued because personally, I start my day with silence and I knew this could be a powerful tool to instill in my students.

The principal proceeded to tell me that she starts the students with just one minute of silence and then increases it by a minute every month, until she had her middle-school students sitting quietly for eight minutes every day. That, in itself, is astonishing, that teenagers can sit quietly for eight minutes without having to be stimulated with electronic devices.

Eagerly, I tried this idea in my classroom and it was extremely beneficial to us all. I will briefly outline how I applied her system and what has worked for me. On the first day of school, as the tornado of the first day starts to come to a close, I tell the students that we are going to sit silently for one minute. Furthermore, I tell them that it doesn't sound like a long time, but the first time I sat quietly for a minute, it seemed like an eternity. I also tell them to expect their mind to wander. This exercise is about just starting to bring our wandering mind back to the present moment. Thus, the more it wanders, the more practice we get bringing it back.

Together, we take three deep breaths and relax our bodies on every exhale. Some students will not breathe deeply, so I tell them to breathe in and count to three, hold it for a second and then breathe out and count to three. Next, I tell the students that rubbing your temples gently as you breathe deeply helps relax the body. Also, I give the students an additional option of tracing the outside of their hand, breathing in as they trace up a finger and out as they trace down a finger.

Next, I tell everyone to get comfortable but sit up straight. Initially, I let students put their heads on their desks, but some would fall asleep, so we don't do that anymore. This is not nap time. Then, I turn out the lights and tell them to sit quietly and try to feel the peace this brings.

After the minute, I ask the students about their experience with one minute of silence. It is always interesting; most of the students feel the peace that silence brings into the classroom. Interestingly, one student described the peaceful feeling as a "light bulb glowing in my belly."

But, I see some students struggle and I try to help those students, telling them it will get easier with practice, like everything in life. I share the fact that sitting quietly was very hard for me at the beginning also and many adults cannot perform this simple task with ease.

Some students can sit quietly from the beginning of this exercise. But others, like Desta, whose story started this chapter, have inquired about what they should do during the silence because their mind wanders. I tell them to compose a gratitude list or take one gratitude deeper, like thinking about what they ate for breakfast and all the people who made that possible.

Other students enjoy contemplating the gratitude of how much technology has gone into any electronic device, including the history and the actual technicians who make each gadget. If your school permits, you may even give the students the option of saying their favorite prayer.

At the end of each month, we vote as a class if they want to elongate our silent time for another minute. This incremental approach seems to work well and *the vote is always overwhelming to increase the silence. Some years, I do get a couple students who vote against it, but perhaps they are the ones who need this quiet time the most. Many of those students who are resisting the silence change their vote as we practice more and get more comfortable with the quiet time.*

Not only does this method work with students, but friends who have tried it have had success. Just like gratitude, if we practice it first and share our experience with our students, it becomes more powerful and effective. At the end of this book, there are websites offering other methods to help students and adults sit quietly and mindfully.

MINDFULNESS IDEAS FOR THE CLASSROOM

In the classroom, we can try to remember to take that long breath before we respond in any stressful situation, whether it is a discipline situation or responding to a challenging email. One friend calls this the "three second cushion," where we take a deep breath and pause for three seconds before we respond.

Three seconds may be extremely hard to wait through and may even seem like an eternity, but that time makes it possible to change the manner in which we respond. Every morning, this friend says to himself, "Today, I will give everyone that I come in contact with a three second cushion." He says this helps him respond with kindness and not from frustration.

Another friend has a little reminder at her computer monitor that says, "Take a breath before sending that email." She says that doing that for the regular emails helps remind her to do this also when she gets an angry email from a parent. Taking that breath enables her to get some perspective and not react without thinking.

Mindfulness and My Silent Retreat

After my first year of teaching, a trusted colleague told me the best way to rejuvenate and recharge was to go on a "silent" retreat. This was a new concept for me. I had been on retreats with friends, but never a silent retreat. I asked my wife what she thought about this and she laughed, saying, "You love to talk so much, you will never make it a whole weekend without talking."

I also had to laugh because she is right: I do love to talk. Teaching is a great profession for "talkers" but after this conversation, I realized I needed to bring some balance into my life and try to embrace silence and mindfulness a little more.

Surprisingly, that first night of silence wasn't bad; in fact, it felt refreshing. The next morning, I faced the first major challenge: breakfast was silent. At first,

I felt very uncomfortable, sitting around other people, all strangers, eating and not communicating, not making that "small talk" that accompanies so many meals. But, after about ten minutes, I got over the initial shock and found myself slowing down and not wolfing my food down, like I do sometimes in my hurry to do something else. Mindfully eating started to feel peaceful and even enjoyable.

As I felt the restorative power of silence throughout the retreat, I made a deal with myself that I would wake up five minutes early and spend that time in silence to begin my day with this mindful and peaceful feeling I was savoring on the retreat.

In addition, I realized that this would help me rejuvenate during the school day. I recognized that I could take a couple minutes on a break, lock my classroom door, and sit quietly, allowing myself to recharge mindfully.

I am glad to say that I enjoyed those five minutes starting every day so much, that I expanded it to ten minutes. Also, I savor those minutes of daily mindful silence in the classroom that I do it more often, finding that I have more energy to teach and enjoy it more after every session.

My students even notice these changes in me. One student said, "You have the best coffee breaks, you must go to Starbucks or somewhere fun because you always come back with a smile and you have more energy." I told him that I use that time to silently recharge. Then, I do it with the students and we all enjoy the positive effects.

We all can find a couple minutes to recharge silently in the classroom and get through the day with a smile, being more effective and enjoying the students much more.

Many of us can't take a weekend from our insanely busy lives to go on a silent retreat, but we can all find a couple hours some weekend to spend in silence, either in our homes or out in nature. Even a few hours can make a world of difference in our lives and in our classrooms.

We do not have to go on an "official" silent retreat to make it effective. I have a friend who will take a day and unplug the phone, turn off all electronic devices, and go into silent mode for a day in her house. She says it is very effective.

If we can embrace silence, even briefly, through all the chatter of the world, we get the profound peace that is so deeply satisfying that it follows us through our busy days. A friend once described that peace as being in "the eye of the hurricane," pandemonium can be going on all around us in the classroom, but we can be at peace, as long as we are centered in silence and mindfulness.

MINDFULNESS CHALLENGE

Take the mindfulness challenge and don't be afraid to try it in the classroom; even starting once a week can make a tremendous difference. More information about organizations that help implement mindfulness in the classroom is in the appendix of this book.

Learning Mindfulness from Superheroes

Recently, at my son's prompting, I sat quietly with my six year old. We both felt very refreshed after our session. I asked him at the end why he wanted to sit quietly. Humorously, he told me that his favorite superhero, Wolverine, sits quietly. I didn't realize that Wolverine could inspire my son to embrace silence, but we never know when positive role models may appear to help us.

STEPPING STONES TO GRATITUDE

1. Mindfulness is a tool that can help us be more balanced, peaceful, and effective in our lives and in our classrooms.
2. Compelling research has shown that students who practice mindfulness improve academically and socially.
3. Research also shows that teachers who are taught mindfulness techniques experience less burnout, lower levels of stress in the classroom, and are able to teach more efficiently.
4. Some techniques to help cultivate mindfulness include focusing on our breathing, taking time to be quiet and mindful, as well as keeping a "half-smile" all day.
5. We can practice mindfulness with our classes by starting with a minute of silence and increasing it slowly.

LET'S TALK ABOUT IT

1. Is mindfulness an effective tool for students and teachers?
2. What does the research say about the efficacy of mindfulness in education?
3. Which mindfulness tools do you think would be most effective for you and your students?

Chapter Nine

Gratitude and Teenagers

Gratitude is a quality similar to electricity; it must be produced and discharged and used up in order to exist at all.

—William Faulkner

When working with the fourth graders and their families on gratitude, one mom laughed and said, "Gratitude works great with the fourth graders, but I doubt you could make my teenager grateful." This was an interesting concern. She is right: no one can make anyone else grateful, but we can introduce, model, and encourage students to try gratitude activities to improve their lives.

Nevertheless, she has a point. Adolescents are sometimes difficult to reach and may pose a challenge to some of our gratitude activities. However, many teenagers and pre-teens that may not appear receptive to gratitude actually open up and experience the positive benefits that gratitude brings into their lives when we take time to give them some choices and independence in their participation.

Adolescents are at a critical crossroads in their lives, when they are seeking to form their own identity and to establish some independence from traditional roles in their families. Consequently, a lack of initial willingness to partake in a family activity like gratitude is understandable. On the other hand, gratitude may help teens at this crucial juncture in many ways, including choosing better friends and taking more positive actions that will ensure their future success.

Moreover, gratitude helps teens build healthier relationships, establish deeper trust, and keep those loving family bonds intact throughout a lifetime, especially during the crucial years. At times, adolescents experience new emotions that are off both ends of the spectrum. Choosing gratitude may even balance out some negative emotions and keep complaining to a minimum.

So, how do we help teens? Let's take a look at the physiology of the adolescent brain, the research, and then some effective activities and options.

THE PHYSIOLOGY OF THE
DEVELOPING TEENAGE BRAIN

If we understand the developing teenage brain, we are more likely to understand teenagers and the possible challenges we may encounter with them. Recent research about the physiology of the adolescent brain can help us appreciate the challenges and the possibilities that lie within their developing brains. Dr. Frances Jensen, head of neuroscience at the University of Pennsylvania, Perelman School of Medicine, published a captivating book about this subject called *The Teenage Brain*.

In this book, Jensen focuses on the prefrontal cortex and shows that this vital part of the teen's brain is not fully developed. Interestingly, this part of the brain is where executive function resides and is the last area to become fully "myelinated." Myelination is the mechanism that insulates and wraps around the actual neurons, increasing the speed of communication between brain cells.

Like a corporate executive, the executive function in the brain has far-reaching implications that will affect the future of a teen. Sometimes in the teenager's life, a decision they make may seem foolish. But, as educators, we can gently guide the teenager and try to remember that this area of the brain is still developing. Although teenagers may appear to be all "grown-up" on the outside, their brains are still developing and myelination is continuing, even into the mid-twenties.

While this may help us understand why adolescents sometimes make apparently impulsive decisions, we need to look at other aspects of their developing brains. As the teenage brain develops, they possess a neuro-plasticity or flexibility to learn and adapt in ways the adult brain may not have anymore.

With regards to gratitude, this is encouraging because the teenager may be more receptive to gratitude, which may result in positive changes in brain development and function. Furthermore, as they practice gratitude, teenagers build neural pathways that can establish patterns that last throughout their lives.

GRATITUDE RESEARCH AND THE TEENAGER

Now, let's take a look at the research. Does scientific investigation show that gratitude works with these students we affectionately call the "hormonally challenged?" In his article, "Pay It Forward," Dr. Robert Emmons conducted research that shows how gratitude may inspire kindness, connections to others, and transformative life changes. All three of these are important to everyone, but may be especially imperative in the teen years, particularly in establishing more healthy social connections.

Another top gratitude researcher, Dr. Jeffrey Froh, conducted a study looking at generosity and gratitude in teenagers. Generosity is important as it helps create positive and healthy relationships. Dr. Froh, along with Dr. Leo Chaplin and his colleagues from the University of Illinois, conducted a two-week study, looking at two groups of adolescents. In the study, one group of adolescents kept a gratitude journal for two weeks, while the other group kept a regular journal with no reference to gratitude for the same two weeks.

At the end of the two weeks, the teens were given ten dollars for their participation in the study. They were also told that they could keep all the money or give some or all of it to charity. Not surprisingly, the teens who kept the gratitude journal donated 60 percent more money than the other group. These results indicate a positive link between gratitude and generosity in teens.

POSITIVE EFFECTS OF GRATITUDE ON TEENAGERS

Furthermore, Dr. Giacomo Bono and Dr. Jeffrey Froh conducted a study, published in the *American Psychological Association Journal*, that found teens who reported high levels of gratitude when entering high school demonstrated less depression and negative emotions, as well as showing greater hope and happiness throughout high school.

What about the teenagers who did not enter high school with high levels of gratitude? If these students worked on becoming more grateful, Dr. Bono reported, "They experienced many of the same improvements in well-being. Moreover, they showed slight reductions overall in delinquency, such as alcohol and drug use, cheating on exams, skipping school, detention and administrative discipline." Additionally, Bono said that this study shows a strong link between gratitude and important life skills, such as cooperation, purpose, creativity, and persistence.

At the conclusion of the four-year period, teens who reported being the most grateful:

• became 15 percent more satisfied with their life overall (at home, at school, with their neighborhood, with their friends, and with themselves).
• became 17 percent happier and more hopeful about their lives.
• experienced a 13 percent drop in negative emotions and a 15 percent drop in depressive symptoms.

Anyone working with teenagers will find hope in these findings. Bono concludes his study with more encouraging words, "More gratitude may be precisely what our society needs to raise a generation that is ready to make a difference in the world."

In a final study published in the *Journal of School Psychology*, Dr. Froh and colleagues had sixth- and seventh-grade students participate in a study that looked at a gratitude intervention of counting blessings. Randomly, students were assigned to a "gratitude, hassles, or a control" condition. For the group that actually counted their blessings, the students reported enhanced optimism and satisfaction with life. Accordingly, the hassles group reported the lowest levels in the same areas.

In conclusion, the study said, "The most significant finding was the robust relationship between gratitude and satisfaction with school experience at both the immediate post-test and three week follow up. Counting blessings seems to be an effective intervention for well-being enhancement in early adolescents."

EXAMPLES OF GRATITUDE
ACTIVITIES WITH TEENAGERS

One suggestion for a gratitude activity for teens comes from an eighth-grade teacher who shared a creative intervention that she calls a "gratitude wall," where students write about things they appreciate about each other on a piece of butcher paper taped to the wall. The teacher shared that her students will share things with her and the class when they are using this gratitude intervention that they would never share otherwise, giving them an opportunity to open up to each other and connect in new ways.

Wisely, she let the students lead this activity and formulate a means to make sure all students were included by keeping track with a student list and writing different student's names on the wall each week. Including the teenagers in setting up this activity created a "buy-in" from her students, helping them take ownership and become intrinsically involved.

In addition, one student suggested that all comments be "real" and not just clichés like, "she is nice" or "he is smart." This challenged the students to think deeper and find those sometimes hidden qualities in others. With a little guidance, she reported that it worked out well. Each year, my colleague conducts this activity with her new students. Happily, she reports that this action is one of the most powerful ways to promote a positive culture in her class throughout the school year.

Another colleague who teaches pre-calculus in high school recently related the way she employs "Kindness Cards." Every Friday, she passes out simple cards to the students. They then use these cards to express a "kindness or gratitude" to someone else in the class. To ensure all students get a card, she assigns students someone to write to. This guarantees that all students will write to all other class members by the end of the semester.

When she first introduced this activity, some of the students said that this is a waste of time and asked if they really had to participate. Interestingly, the students who complained the most at first were also the ones who benefited the most from this exercise. One of these students kept the cards in a special place as the school year progressed and reported that these cards helped get him through the tough parts of the year. Of all the activities this teacher tried, this was one of the most effective and long-lasting.

Additionally, Dr. Christine Carter, an expert on adolescent education, suggests teens focus on altruistic action, finding ways to help others and practice kindness. She states, "Helping others evokes feelings of gratitude, compassion, and confidence in people of any age." One idea she reports is to ask teenagers in our classes or our families to find an organization that represents a cause they believe in, and then volunteer. For those who are extremely busy, even one day a month can make a tremendous difference in an adolescent's life.

Another idea is to have teens write gratitude notes to adults in their lives who have helped them. This could be a teacher, coach, member of the clergy, or administrator. Furthermore, if a teacher from their elementary or middle school had an impact on a teenager's life, the teenager could volunteer some time in that teacher's classroom, putting their gratitude into action.

DON'T GIVE UP

When trying to get gratitude to work with teenagers in our classrooms and families, don't give up if it does not work immediately. Keep trying and give them options and independence. Include them in researching new gratitude activities and let them lead us in new directions. Remember that teens may not express gratitude the way younger children do, but they still feel it and need it.

STEPPING STONES TO GRATITUDE:

1. Teenagers may pose a special challenge to the implementation of gratitude in our classrooms and families.
2. Adolescent brains are still developing and the last area to fully develop is the prefrontal cortex, where executive decisions are made.

3. Gratitude activities do work with teens; giving them choices and independence helps.
4. Even if we are not successful initially, don't give up. Some teens will respond after a little time.

LET'S TALK ABOUT IT

1. What activities would work the most effectively to make teenagers try gratitude in their lives?
2. What are some of the biggest challenges to getting teenagers to use gratitude?
3. What potential benefits does gratitude hold for adolescents?

Chapter Ten

Enlisting the Support of Family

Piglet noticed that even though he had a very small heart, it could hold a rather large amount of gratitude.

—A.A. Milne, from "Winnie-the-Pooh"

Reflect on your present blessings, on which every man has many, not on your past misfortunes, of which all men have some.

—Charles Dickens

Getting families involved with the action of gratitude is imperative to making it a lasting part of the lives of our students. Also, by incorporating the family in the gratitude journey, we help spread gratitude out to our communities, and we are helping to reshape the world.

Enlisting the support of families does not need to be challenging or complicated. Sometimes it just flows naturally. Here is a remarkable example of gratitude spreading to a family from Emma, an extraordinary ten-year-old student. Her story can help us see how gratitude may blossom in a family at a time it is needed. This is the text from an actual note that Emma and her mother presented me, along with a beautiful leather bound journal:

Mr. Griffith,

Thank you for the great year! I'll never forget you. You are the best teacher I've ever had. Without you, I would have never known about the "Attitude of Gratitude." You will always be at the top of my gratitude list.

Your student,
Emma

Mr. Griffith,

I can't thank you enough for the year you gave Emma. I have watched her grow in so many ways and many of them I have you to thank. I especially want to thank you for the "Attitude of Gratitude." I have to be honest, when she gave me the gratitude journal for Christmas, I was a little wary. But, out of love for Emma, I did it. The journal has become very special to me.

Please use this journal, as it says on the front, "Write with your heart" about all your special teaching moments. When you are having a hard day, look back and remember all of the students and families you have touched through the years as you have touched us. Good luck and God bless you. See you in the halls.

Cathy (Emma's Mom)

After presenting the notes, the mom told me how Emma had saved up her money and went out and purchased gratitude journals for the entire family. At the dinner table at Christmas, she presented them to everyone saying, "Mr. Griffith says that what we focus on in life grows, and I want us to focus on all the good things in life. So here are gratitude journals we can all start and work on as a family."

It turns out Emma's mom had just started nursing school and things were stressful around the house. As it says in the note, at first, she was leery and thought this would just be another obligation in her busy life, but as the family began writing and sharing their gratitudes together, they established a new family tradition that transformed their family forever.

GRATITUDE IN ACTION: FAMILY GRATITUDE ALBUMS

In our classroom this year, we began a "Gratitude Album" that students get to take home and decorate. This activity is a great infusion of appreciation into the families of our students. Each individual student takes the album home for a week and is challenged to creatively show how they practice gratitude to make it part of their family's life. Each student is given one huge page in the book to beautify with family gratitude. This is a gratitude activity we can practice in the classroom and also encourage families to keep their own personal family gratitude album.

When the students complete their page, they share it with the class by showing the lovely artwork and telling everyone how their family helped them demonstrate and assimilate gratitude into their family lives. Finally, they express how their family is enjoying the benefits of gratitude.

An interesting byproduct of this activity is that some siblings of the students in our class started creating their own "Gratitude Artwork" and beginning their own personal gratitude journals. After finishing their family's page in our "Gratitude Album," one student's younger brother said he hoped to have one million gratitudes in his journal by the time he reached my fourth-grade class.

Remarkably, this younger brother was only in first grade, so we encouraged him and gently reminded him that with gratitude, quality is more important than quantity and going deeper into each gratitude is important. Still, we told him to keep trying to be grateful and maybe even try different gratitude activities to prevent gratitude "fatigue." He said he would try to come up with some of his very own gratitude activities. We can't wait to see what he creates and what gratitude creates in his life and the life of his family.

EXAMPLES OF FAMILY GRATITUDE ALBUMS

On the pages of our class's gratitude family album, members of student's families shared what they were grateful for, opening up discussions that continue in those families. One student drew his family on vacation and wrote, "I am grateful for the love and fun we share as a family. When we are on vacation, we get to try new things and laugh together." This student's mom told me that her son is seeing new and positive things in the world since beginning to practice gratitude.

Another creative student made her page a "Family Mission" to be more grateful. This was expressed as a "journey" the family would take each day, to see the good and positive in each other and in the world. Each family member wrote about what they are grateful for now and how they will all make gratitude their personal mission. They committed to do more things together as a family, including eating dinner together as much as possible and begin it with a prayer where each member expresses a gratitude. The artwork on this page expressed the love and commitment the family is sharing to successfully complete their "gratitude mission."

GRATITUDE VISIT

Another potent tool to help families exercise gratitude in their lives is the "Gratitude Visit." This was mentioned earlier in the book, but here it takes on a new dimension as the family does it together and multiplies the benefits. With this gratitude visit, family members write a letter to someone who has earned their gratitude, but which had not yet been expressed. This could be a relative, teacher, family friend, or anyone who has helped enrich their lives. The family delivers this letter to the person and expresses their gratitude face to face.

For families that have tried this, it becomes an indelible memory, with benefits for all participating family members.

When practicing this as a family, members can send letters to anyone, but often they choose family members as recipients of their appreciation. One student wrote a letter to her older sister in college. Then, the family took a special trip to visit the sister to deliver the letter. Tears of joy came from everyone as the student relayed a list of all the things her big sister had done for her that have made a tremendous difference in her life. According to the family, this action brought the two of them closer and their relationship keeps growing and becoming richer.

GRATITUDE FACEBOOK PAGE

Here is another simple example of enlisting the family in a gratitude activity utilizing social media. A colleague began a Facebook page where students and families would share the gratitude going on in their lives. Many families happily posted on the Facebook page and benefited from this easy activity.

The beautiful and persuasive aspect of this action, as with all the activities included in this chapter, is to see how appreciation shared in the family seems to reshape and invigorate the family with a new and positive sense of each other and the world. In addition, when people view the Facebook page and see how gratitude enables families to connect to each other and the community in new ways, it motivates them to integrate gratitude into their lives.

GRATITUDE BOARD ON REFRIGERATOR

Here is another unpretentious yet effective idea for families: put a dry erase board on the refrigerator dedicated to writing gratitudes. A student who had originally put some sticky notes on his family's refrigerator and was disappointed when they fell off or got lost came up with the idea for the dry erase board. He said that in his family, people seemed go to the refrigerator many times a day. In fact, he humorously said his teenage brother visited the fridge about a hundred times or more daily. Thus, a dry erase board would allow family members to express their gratitude in a place that they would often see and they would be reminded to maintain a positive attitude.

This sounded like a novel way for his family to express their thankfulness, but how does it work with erasing the board? The student said that they kept adding gratitudes to the board for a week and then on Sunday, they would erase it to allow for new gratitudes. Even the youngest member of the family, who was only three, was getting into the act by asking others to hold her up as she drew what she was thankful for.

GRATITUDE QUESTIONS AT THE END OF THE DAY

Another creative family compiled some gratitude questions that they would ask at dinner or bedtime. They filled a jar with slips of paper and a variety of questions, like "Who were you most grateful for today and why?" or "What are you grateful for that you ate today, and how many people had to work to get that food to you?" Once a question was used, they would throw it away and refill the jar periodically. The children enjoyed this so much that they would request the gratitude question if the parents forgot.

GRATITUDE STONE

An additional activity to try with our families is the "gratitude stone." Have everyone in your family pick a stone from nature or even buy some small stones from a craft store. Then, paint it colorfully and write the word, "Gratitude" or something else meaningful on it. After it dries, have family members carry the stone in their pockets, purses, briefcases, or school bags and every time they see the "gratitude" stone or feel it, they should think of one thing they are thankful for.

FAMILY PHOTOS

When speaking with Dr. Jeffrey Froh, a leading gratitude researcher, he said that the traditional gratitude list doesn't always work for him, so he strategically placed photos of his family and every time he saw one of these photos, he reminded himself of something he was grateful for about his family. This works beautifully for him and as we try this, it can help us grow in gratitude for our families.

TWO-COLUMN GRATITUDE LIST

Here is a spin on the traditional gratitude list, make a two-column gratitude list. In the first column, simply write the gratitude, but in the second column, write an action to take to show how grateful we are. When composing the second column, we are forced to take gratitude from an emotion to an action and live gratitude in our lives and with our families.

STEPPING STONES TO GRATITUDE

1. By enlisting the help of families with gratitude, we are cementing this practice in our families and also spreading it out to the world.
2. We can experiment with a variety of simple yet powerful gratitude activities for students and their families.
3. Putting gratitude into action as a family can change our students, our families, and our world.

LET'S TALK ABOUT IT

1. Why is it important to try to spread gratitude to our families and the families of our students?
2. What are some gratitude activities that would work in your family or with your student's families?
3. Can you think of any other family gratitude activities that would be an enjoyable way to express gratitude?

Chapter Eleven

Keeping Gratitude Fresh and Energized throughout the School Year

At times our own light goes out and is rekindled by a spark from another person. Each of us has cause to think with deep gratitude of those who have lighted the flame within us.

—Albert Schweitzer

Teaching is challenging and the school year may seem very long. In fact, the school year may even seem like a combination of a marathon race and a rollercoaster ride, if it were possible to combine those two things. Recently, a colleague said the school year does seem like a marathon race, but they want us to sprint all 26.2 miles. This is where practicing gratitude in our classroom gives us the extra energy to pull us through the school year, especially when we hit our "wall" and can't seem to go on.

———————————————— ⌘ ————————————————

Don't Make Me Pull this Car Over

A couple years ago, as students were bickering in my class toward the end of the school year, I said, "You two get along; don't make me pull this car over." That broke the tension and made us all laugh. I realized that the school year is sometimes like a long ride in a car. At the start, everyone is friends, but by the end, everyone is getting on each other's nerves. So what can we do to help us all stay refreshed and get along through the school year? Apply more gratitude. This chapter includes some ideas.

———————————————— ⌘ ————————————————

MORE EFFECTIVE GRATITUDE IDEAS

One effective gratitude idea is to write a gratitude note about our students to their parents. In his book, *Thanks, A 21-Day Program*, Robert Emmons mentions some intriguing research that shows the power of a simple note of gratitude. In restaurants, when a waiter or waitress wrote a simple two word "Thank you" on the bill or drew a happy face, they received as much as an 11 percent higher tip.

As teachers, we can also utilize this potent tool by taking the time to write a quick gratitude note to the parents of our students. A colleague suggested this and even gave me a template to make the notes with some beautiful clip art showing a big happy face. As mentioned earlier, these notes are more effective when handwritten and should be sent by traditional mail, as it is more powerful for the parents and students to receive a letter rather than just an email or text. The students and parents truly enjoy the novelty of receiving a real letter in the mailbox.

This action gives us an opportunity to reflect and build an awareness of gratitude in our lives and our classrooms. By taking time to notice and articulate something we are grateful for about each student, we cultivate a culture of appreciation in our classrooms and at our schools. This note may be something as simple as "I wanted to take a moment to tell you how grateful I am to have Joseph in my class this year. Joseph is a kind and intelligent young man. Just the other day, he helped another student pick up her books on the way out of the classroom."

Obviously, these notes will be easier to write for some students than others. But we can find something positive about every student. This is an exercise that also helps us focus on the positive attributes of all our students, especially the challenging ones.

Gregory

One year, after these notes were sent to parents, a student came in and said, "Mr. Griffith, I don't know why you sent that note to my Mom, but she put it on our fridge and made a copy to send to Grandma. Every time I go to the fridge at home, I feel good about being in your class and coming to school. I never really felt that before." This came from a student who struggled in many areas, but improved dramatically by the end of the school year. This little investment of my time brought prodigious results.

SECRET GRATITUDE PARTNERS/SPIES

In our class, we do many activities to stay energized with gratitude. In this next activity, we put a twist on the idea of writing a gratitude letter by assigning the students a "secret gratitude partner." We tell them they have to be "gratitude spies" and observe the other student to find something to write about, telling the other student why they are grateful for him or her.

Then, at the end of the week, each student writes a letter, telling his or her "secret gratitude partner" why he or she is appreciated. When we reveal the gratitude partners, it is a joyful day. We switch partners and ensure that every student is paired with every other one. This definitely raises class morale and brings some fresh air into the long car ride of the school year.

IDENTIFYING SURVIVAL MODE

In addition to utilizing a variety of gratitude activities, we need to be able to identify when we are in survival mode to ensure that we stay energized throughout the long school year. How do teachers get in survival mode? Well, teaching is a demanding job. With all the responsibilities and demands on our time and energy, it is easy to feel like we do not have any energy left for anyone, including ourselves. Like other problems, the first step is becoming aware of the situation and then we can take action to break free from it. Here is good news: gratitude and some other simple actions help us get out and stay out of survival mode.

People in survival mode are just barely getting by day to day. When we are in survival mode, we do the minimum because we do not feel like we have the energy to do more. There seems to be no joy and not much gratitude, light, or laughter in our lives. As a teacher, when we are in survival mode not only do we affect our lives but also the lives of our many students. Sadly, getting stuck in survival mode leads to burnout and may contribute to the high attrition rate for the profession of teaching.

Naturally, we all get run down and slip into survival mode sometimes. If we are sick or going through a major change, like moving, having a baby, or having a major family crisis, we may enter survival mode. That is okay. But, it is not okay to stay there. The next question is, "How do we get out of survival mode?"

GETTING AND STAYING OUT OF SURVIVAL MODE

We begin to rise out of survival mode by asking the question that Parker Palmer, an educator and writer, poses, "What do I need to do right now, to water the root of inner wisdom that makes work fruitful?" When we are in survival mode, we actually are afforded an opportunity to look at our life and try to make new priorities, taking care of ourselves in new ways. Now we will look at some tools to enable us to make the essential changes to get out and stay out of survival mode.

TRY NEW EXPERIENCES/WELCOME MISTAKES AS LEARNING EXPERIENCES

One of the first things to think about is simple: don't get caught in a rut. Survival mode is one of the worst of all ruts. The only difference between a rut and a grave is how deep it is. Make opportunities to be spontaneous, adventurous, and playful every day in and out of the classroom. Our students and children give lessons in this daily. Also, try to get out of your comfort zones. Remember that the worst that can happen is that we will make a new mistake instead of repeating the same one that hasn't work for us in the past.

You are Not Making Enough Mistakes

I had an insightful supervisor once who said to me, "You are not trying enough new things in your job." I asked him how he knew that and he said, "I can tell you are not trying new things because you are not making mistakes. I know you are a bit of perfectionist, but don't let this paralyze you and don't be afraid to make some mistakes. That is how we learn. Now, don't get me wrong, it is okay to make mistakes when we try new things, but learn from those mistakes and try not to repeat them." This gave me the courage to try many novel things and present fresh ideas at that job. I grew in many new and unexpected ways.

Don't listen to the lie that we don't have enough time or energy. New experiences create energy and allow us more time for everything. Fearlessly try new things and learn from those mistakes in order to grow out of survival mode.

Learning and Being Nourished by Students

As a teacher, one of the greatest joys is learning from my students as we integrate the practice of gratitude in our lives. This allows nourishment from the students that keeps me refreshed all year. Daily, I am given the opportunity to interact and connect with my students as we teach each other. When I realized that I could learn from and be energized by my students, I had my first "A-ha" moment and that changed everything in my classroom. This awareness brought wonder and passion into my teaching. The paradigm of teacher/students is still constantly being flipped.

Recently, I ran into a mom whose son was in my class six years ago and is now in high school. She told me that he was so excited about writing a gratitude list that he came home and wrote a list of one hundred gratitudes after his first day in my class.

However, gratitude does not make every day perfect in my classroom. I still have challenging days, where gratitude is hard to find and things irritates me more easily. But I still have a choice to look for gratitude. On those challenging days, when I write a gratitude list, I feel a little better. This exercise helps me become a better teacher and stay out of survival mode.

PRACTICE RADICAL GRATITUDE

This book says it in so many ways, but let's put it succinctly here—*practice radical gratitude.* Take gratitude to the next level by seeing the world and the classroom through the lens of gratitude and share it in new and "radical" ways. Survival mode blocks us from seeing all the positive things in our lives. We can cultivate an awareness of the many gifts in our lives and become aware of new gifts as the school year progresses.

No matter how busy life feels, take a moment to try one of the gratitude activities from this book. One place to start is to realize that a vast majority of the population of the planet would change places with most of us in an instant. Then, look around at all the things we take for granted daily, including the ability to read and communicate, connecting with others in so many ways. This book is helping us communicate in a way that many people in this world do not have.

Remember that what we focus on in life contributes to how we feel about ourselves, our teaching, and our lives. Thus, focus on all the good that we have and watch it all grow. Take more action: write a gratitude letter to someone new and deliver it in person. We have written about the benefits for our students and their families, now we need to try it ourselves. Let that person know how appreciated he or she is. And by giving a little, we help ourselves get out and stay out of survival mode.

Alexis and Radical Gratitude

Alexis was a student who taught me a number of lessons, but the most powerful lesson she embodied was persistence coupled with gratitude. In class, she would diligently complete her work and then ask for extra math work. I would give her math drills, word problems, and math enrichment exercises. Taking these extra assignments, she would happily smile.

Then, one day I looked at her and said, "It is so good to see how much you love math." She looked surprised and said, "Oh no, math is my hardest subject. After I heard you say that we should be grateful for the things that challenge us in life, I told myself I would work really hard on my hardest subject, math. Maybe with some extra work, I can turn it into my best subject." She succeeded and it did not take long. She was soon one of the best math students in the class.

This lesson was instantly applicable in my life and classroom. At times, I tend to shy away from activities that I do not think I am good at. But this student demonstrated that diving in and putting some extra effort into a challenging area will bring success. I still need to remind myself of this when I am confronted, almost daily, with areas in life that I might avoid instead of embracing. This is practicing Radical Gratitude, when I can see the gift in the challenges in life and then grow from them.

Yesterday, my son said, "Daddy, come draw with me." I almost said, "I am not a good artist." But, I have said this repeatedly. In fact, I have said it so much, it had become automatic. Thankfully, I caught myself that time. Instead, I sat down, grabbed a crayon, and completed a self-portrait, enjoying every second.

HELP OTHERS/GIVE FREELY

In the classroom and in the world, when we help others in big and small ways, we are helping ourselves stay rejuvenated all year. When we partake of altruistic actions, we are taking the action of gratitude that empowers us to feel the profound joy of giving freely with no expectations. It all comes back to us in countless ways.

Altruistic giving has been shown to increase positive neurotransmitters in the giver, receiver, and anyone observing the act of giving. People who volunteer or care for others consistently are happier and less depressed. In her book *Raising Happiness*, Dr. Christine Carter writes about the "Helper's High" we get when we give of ourselves. She describes this as a "distinct physical sensation associated with helping others." Anthony de Mello, a Jesuit priest, presented this as an interesting paradox. He said, "Charity is really self-interest masquerading under the form of altruism. . . . I give myself the pleasure of pleasing others."

So, give to others, practice those random, yet thoughtful, acts of kindness and enjoy the benefits this brings. One simple suggestion is to tell someone at work how much we appreciate them. This could be a quick email or telling them face-to-face. Even better, do someone a good turn today, don't get found out, and feel the profound joy this brings.

FORGIVE/LET GO OF RESENTMENTS

One diametrically opposed action to gratitude is harboring resentments. Many times, we do not consciously build these resentments, but we are stuck in a habit. We need to realize that resentments only hurts us and keeps us stuck in survival mode. One saying is that resentments are like stray cats; if we don't feed them, they go away. Another wise saying is, "Don't let others rent free space in our heads." We can forgive and let go.

If we let go a little, we get a little relief. If we let go a lot, we get a lot of relief. And if we let go completely, we are free, truly free to feel and share gratitude with our students and the world. This simple action will keep us energized in the classroom throughout the school year as we are tempted to build new resentments for people who challenge us. We can actually learn from these people; they are our "teachers."

My Student is my Teacher

Early on in my career, I had one student that challenged me and presented a "problem" in an interesting manner. Then a colleague helped change my perspective as they both taught me a valuable lesson.

This student would watch as I wrote on the white board and raise her hand with a little smile on her face. When I called on her, she would correct me saying things like, "Mr. Griffith, you spelled 'millennium' wrong." On that particular day, I was tired and frustrated and I did not take this statement very well. In fact, you might say I was "ungrateful" that morning for the student noticing my mistake and pointing it out in front of the class.

On my first break, I stormed into the teacher's lunchroom and saw a trusted colleague. I told her what had happened and said that this student was being very disrespectful for pointing this out in front of the entire class. I said that this problem was ruining my day.

She smiled knowingly, as good friends do at these moments, looked at me, and said, "Wait a minute, aren't you Mr. Gratitude?" This made me laugh and eased the tension. She went on to say, "That is one of those situations that you can complain about and build up a resentment over or you could change it into something positive. That student had to be paying close attention to find the errors you make. You might think about giving students a reward for finding the errors. Then, if you make an error, you can tell them you were just testing them."

We both smiled and my resentment started to soften. My friend went on, "You just started doing a gratitude list with your students. Maybe that student should be at the top of your gratitude list because she is teaching you to turn problems into solutions."

After lunch, I went back to my classroom and told the students that every day, I would be hiding at least one mistake on the board for them to find, making it a game. If a student found a mistake, they would get a little reward and could make a suggestion for an embedded error for the next day.

Immediately, all the students started paying closer attention to everything I wrote. They started noticing when I purposely wrote something wrong on the board, like a misspelled word or a grammar or punctuation error. And if I did make an error and they noticed, we could laugh it off as something I "purposely" did.

At the end of the school year, when this class took a standardized test, the scores for editing and correcting punctuation and grammar went through the roof. That one student, who started this entire change in my perspective, scored at the college level in this area and this was for a fourth-grade student. I realized that I could have squashed her talent, but a friend reminded me to look at this from an angle of gratitude. And that turned this into a moment we both learned from and I still grow from.

WORK THROUGH FEAR

Fear blocks out gratitude, drains our precious energy, keeps us stuck in survival mode, and holds us back from truly living our lives or being the best teacher we can be. We can generally unmask our fears by asking two questions:

1. Are we afraid we are going to lose something we have?
2. Are we afraid we won't get something we want?

Once we are aware of the fear, then we can focus on some actions that we can take to work through the fear. For example, if we are afraid we won't have enough money, we can do some research or reach out to others for ideas about saving money or generating some income. It is okay to feel the fear, but we cannot allow it to paralyze us.

Walk through the fear and feel it dissipate. Also, if we share a fear with a friend or colleague we trust, it feels like we cut it in half. There is power in just getting it out of our heads and letting it go. Writing about it by keeping a journal can also help us keep perspective on fear.

QUIT TAKING IT PERSONALLY (ACRONYM: Q-TIP)

Another thing that blocks out gratitude and lowers us into survival mode is taking things personally. As teachers, we pour so much of ourselves into our classrooms and our lessons. This is one of the joys of teaching, but it can also make it hard to not take comments about our teaching personally. Still, we can protect ourselves with some simple ideas.

First of all, most comments are not personal and even when comments are made that seem designed to hurt us, we can try not to take it personally. If that person is really trying to hurt us, we do not have to allow them to succeed. It is okay to create healthy boundaries, but we do not need to waste extra time and energy by trying to extract an apology or get revenge.

If we inject gratitude into this equation of not taking things personal as teachers, we may even grow from the comment made by a parents, colleagues, or administrators. Some effective refinements made in the classroom can stem from comments from parents. But, if we take these suggestions personally and get defensive, instead of trying to see if there is some substance to them, the opportunity is missed.

At a recent faculty meeting at another school, a principal actually passed out Q-Tips and went over this idea with the staff. She suggested that everyone carry the Q-Tip around and remember to not take things so personally. They can throw it away when it has become a habit.

KEEP A SENSE OF HUMOR

Humor is a powerful way to stay fresh and rejuvenated throughout the long school year. Humor and gratitude are related because when we are grateful, we do see more humor in our lives and we don't take ourselves so seriously. We can remember that there are very serious things in life, but we can temper that with a sense of humor about ourselves and the situations we are presented with in the classrooms. By keeping a sense of humor, we can learn to laugh at ourselves in stressful situations and keep some balance, gratitude, and a positive perspective.

Encouraging healthy humor in our classrooms and lives is an affirmative step to take into our classrooms. We can show this by laughing at ourselves when we make a mistake in front of the class. Thus, we are modeling this healthy behavior for the students, reminding them to learn from mistakes, but not to beat themselves up or take it all too seriously.

Micah the Comedian

I had a student, Micah, who had a wonderful and mischievous sense of humor. This student had a reputation for being a real disruption to classes with his "inappropriate humor." At the beginning of the school year, he tried to disrupt my class by blurting out something that got the entire class laughing but also got us all way off track. Instantly, I tried to think how this challenge and potential year-long battle could be turned into something positive.

Looking through the lens of gratitude, I saw this boy was funny, yet he felt like he needed attention. So I told him, "If you can stay quiet all day, I will give you two minutes at the end of the day to do a comedy routine." He got excited. He asked if he could work up a five-minute routine, have his friend help him write material, and perform on Friday afternoon, so we would all have something to look forward to.

I agreed and never had a problem with him for the rest of the school year. Friday afternoon comedy routines became something we all looked forward to. He did one routine on the spelling bee and another on cafeteria food. Both were hilarious and stayed within the boundaries of what was appropriate. As I keep these moments of gratitude fresh in my mind, I create a joy that changes those insurmountable problems in the classroom into challenges that help me grow.

CHOOSE KINDNESS, ALWAYS

Kindness and gratitude are inextricably intertwined and fuel each other. We should remember to be kind to ourselves and others in all circumstances. One of the hardest things to do in this world is to be kind when someone else is not kind to us. Today, right now, we can all look for a situation in our lives when we are presented with negativity and choose to be kind and even be grateful for the opportunity to grow. This is hard, but it reaps great rewards.

Moreover, we are given these types of opportunities all the time. It may be in our families, at our schools, or even driving. In any of these situations, don't be afraid to look into the other person's eyes, smile, and respond with kindness. Feel the true strength in authentic kindness. See how this makes us feel and the power it has to transform a situation, improving our lives immediately.

GET THROUGH THE SCHOOL YEAR WITH A SMILE

Lastly, these suggestions may seem daunting, but we don't have to try everything at once. As the school year progresses and we need to get energized, try the easiest of these tips to get unstuck and feel refreshed. Then, try something else from this chapter to revitalize and keep out of survival mode. If something doesn't work, remember that one mistake is not a failure but a step to learning. Keep trying and reach out for help. We can do this; we can get through the year with a smile.

What We Leave Behind

At a graduation ceremony last year, one speaker said, "Although you will physically leave this school, part of you will always stay at this school." I really liked that idea. After the graduation ceremony, when we returned to the classroom, one thoughtful girl raised her hand and said, "What will I leave in this classroom after I am gone?"

As I pondered this compelling question, I realized that I could not immediately articulate what specifically she would leave. I looked at her smiling face and told her, "You will leave your smile in the classroom and also in my heart." She looked up and said, "What about my intelligence?" I told her that not only would her intelligence stay with me, but her deep and original questions would resound in my mind and in the minds of her classmates. She laughed and said, "What about my gratitude?" Assuredly, her sense of growing gratitude will always stay with me and light up our classroom even in her physical absence.

At last, I felt like we were getting at the heart of the question. We all leave indelible imprints on each other. I have been teaching for more than ten years and have had the extreme pleasure of teaching over five hundred students, and it is wonderful to know that they have all left their mark on my soul.

What the students leave with me, their imprints on my soul:

- *Genuine gratitude and kindness in all situations in life*
- *Hope for mankind when I see their indomitable spirit*
- *A free pass into their magical worlds, full of love, wonder, play, laughter, and innocence*
- *A chance to see the world through their nascent and hopeful eyes*
- *A reminder to be in the moment where everything is fresh and new*

And what I hope to leave with my students:

- *A thirst for knowledge and the exhilaration of learning*
- *A sense of awe and an awareness of the true strength of kindness*
- *An openness and vulnerability paired with resilience*
- *The gift of music, as it opens up parts of the soul that only music can reach*
- *The idea that we never have a bad day, we just have a bad attitude*
- *The difference between an adventure and an ordeal is our outlook, which we should always temper with gratitude*
- *The ability to experience a profound and growing gratitude for this world and everything in it, as well as some tools to explore that gratitude and to take it to deeper levels, sharing it with the world*

STEPPING STONES TO GRATITUDE

1. By keeping gratitude fresh in our classrooms, we can remain energized through the school year.
2. Stay invigorated throughout the school year by being aware of survival mode and the ways to get out of it.
3. Use the following activities to stay grateful and vital in the classroom:
   - Try new experiences and learn from mistakes.
   - Help others inside and outside classroom.
   - Work through fear.
   - Quit taking it personally (Q-TIP).
   - Choose kindness, especially when challenged.
   - Keep a sense of humor.

LET'S TALK ABOUT IT

1. What can we do to remain invigorated throughout the school year?
2. What is survival mode and how does it relate to gratitude?
3. How do people get stuck in survival mode?
4. Which strategy in this chapter would work best for you or your colleagues?

Chapter Twelve

Remaining Teachable with Gratitude

People will forget what you said. People will forget what you did. But people will never forget how you made them feel.

—Maya Angelou

In life, as well as in the field of education, little things make an enormous difference. Remaining teachable with gratitude may seem like one of those little things, but by practicing gratitude in its many forms and weaving it into our classrooms as our educational careers progress, we will experience continual growth and we may even find some unexpected joy.

LISTENING WITH AN OPEN HEART

To stay teachable with gratitude, we need to improve our listening skills. Listening fundamentally relates to gratitude because if we are truly grateful for our students and colleagues, we will listen and be more attentive to them. Most school days are extremely busy with many tasks to undertake simultaneously. This sometimes makes it difficult to give individual students or colleagues our sustained attention and really listen to them. But, this is one of the most important things we can do every day. Here is an example.

Sarah

I had discipline problems with a girl one year that I will call Sarah. She had a big and forceful personality. It seemed that she was a natural leader of the students, but much of that leading took the students off task and made teaching a challenge.

Then, one day, I remembered the advice of a mentor. The mentor said that if we have a student who is a discipline problem, we should take a few minutes first thing each morning to attend to that student, giving him or her our undivided attention, listening deeply. We may do this by asking the student how his or her night was or how we can be of help. This daily time devoted to the student gives the attention he or she may be seeking with the negative behavior and help forge a new and positive relationship.

When I started doing this, Sarah made a dramatic and surprising turnaround. Quickly, after a few of these brief discussions, she became a model student and a positive leader. One day, she said, "Mr. Griffith, can I be your personal assistant?" This made me smile. I told her I had never had a "personal assistant" in the classroom and she could be the first. In addition, I told her that many executives pay top dollar for such a privilege. She actually had many skills that I never would have uncovered, and the rest of the school year went so much smoother, just because I tried something new, really listening and trying to remain "teachable."

GRATITUDE CONFERENCES

In my classroom, we conduct monthly gratitude conferences. A gratitude conference is when each individual student meets for a couple minutes with the teacher. This gives the teacher an opportunity to tell each student something the teacher is grateful for about that student. More importantly, the teacher asks the student for anything the teacher can help with in the classroom.

Some students say everything is going great and they don't need any help. But here is the power of this action: it gives students an opportunity to express things privately that they may not be able to say in front of the class. Many students have utilized this chance to talk about concerns that might have never been addressed.

With all the demands on our time in the classroom, this may seem just one more thing to do. But by doing it once a month, it doesn't take that much time. In fact, a colleague can come in and watch the class as we take students in the hall for their conference. With a class of twenty-eight students, it really takes less than an hour. This small time investment is well worth it.

In fact, after conducting the first Gratitude Conference of the year, students are told that they can request an extra conference anytime they need it. This opens up the communication and ensures students that we are available for them whenever they need us.

In these conferences, students have voiced concerns about academic areas as well as interpersonal problems. Many problems are small and instantly fixed. However, other problems require help from school counselors or the administration. Students are always reminded that we can work through this together. At the end of the school year, when we solicit feedback from students, these conferences are always at the top of their lists.

GRATITUDE LETTERS IN THE CLASSROOM

In our classroom, to help us all remain teachable with gratitude, we write each other gratitude letters, practicing our writing skills and expressing how much we appreciate each other. We start this after spring break, when we need to build class morale. Making sure all students take part in this activity, we keep a list of the students' letters to ensure everyone writes to everyone.

In addition, we remind the students to include why they are grateful for the other students in the letters, being as specific as possible. Gratitude is again a conscious decision for us as we keep building a positive culture and staying focused on the "good" in each other. Attempting to expand our English skills, we make a list of the "weaker" words and worm them out, like "nice" and "smart," putting them on a "banned" word list. We make a list of more powerful words to use in the letters. Furthermore, we even try to include a "strong verb" and a "quality adjective." We give the students a word list to assist the process and let them generate some of their own powerful words to make the gratitude letter more meaningful and fun.

After the year is over and we are on the other side of the finish line of the school year, exhausted but hopefully satisfied, this is a time for us to celebrate, reflect, and refine our teaching. In our class, we ask the students to reflect on the school year and write a special gratitude letter to someone who has especially helped them throughout the year. The letter is meant to be read at the beginning of summer break and then displayed somewhere the student can enjoy it all summer long.

Sometimes, that letter goes to a friend in the classroom. Surprisingly, that letter often goes to someone else who was not considered a "friend" to begin the school year, but who now feels a new relationship that has been built in our classroom. This unexpected gratitude builds the social fabric throughout the classroom and sets up a wonderful, supportive community in our classroom. Gratitude does help the students grow with social capital as these bonds grow beyond the end of the school year.

———————————————— ✖✖✖ ————————————————

Class Gratitude Book

Last year, the generous and helpful parents and the students made a class grati-
tude book, with each student answering two questions:

1. What were you most grateful for this year in Mr. Griffith's class?
2. What makes Mr. Griffith such a great and grateful teacher?

One girl wrote that what makes me a great and grateful teacher is that I spent
two weeks teaching her long division and would not let her give up, telling her
that I was grateful that she kept trying. She even quoted one of my favorite say-
ings when a student is struggling, "Confusion can be the beginning of learning
if you don't give up."

Finally, my gratitude grows as I read this book when I need a little pick me
up, seeing that students, parents, and colleagues helped me when the marathon
race of the school year seemed too much and I hit my "wall."

At the end of the book, the parents got together and answered the two ques-
tions. One said, "You are a special teacher because you lead the students in
your example of teaching and living with gratitude in everything you do."
Another parent said that the balance of discipline and fun makes a successful
classroom. I agree and try to give the students love and boundaries, focusing
on the positive.

Gratitude helps make that possible. Another parent wrote, "Mr. Griffith gives
of his heart to the students and makes them feel important by honoring them
individually." As teachers, we should connect with a student's heart before
challenging their brains.

———————————————— ✖✖✖ ————————————————

BE A GIVER AND NOT A TAKER
IN THE CLASSROOM AND IN LIFE

If we want to remain teachable with gratitude, we can endeavor to be a
"giver" in the classroom. Once at a talk, the speaker said he doesn't like
to "pigeon-hole" people or minimize them by classifying them, but he still
divides everyone in the world into two groups. He asked us all if we could
guess the two groups. Someone guessed "Winners/Losers"; someone else
guessed "Nice/Mean." Neither answer was right. He said he can put everyone
in one of two groups: "Givers" and "Takers."

Moreover, he went on to delineate the characteristics of each group and gratitude was always present with the "Givers" for the following reasons. First of all, when we practice gratitude in our lives, we can't help but be givers in many ways. People who are grateful givers are happier because they are thinking about others and not so focused on themselves, their problems, or making everything work out exactly as they think they need it to be to achieve happiness. Finally, people practicing grateful altruism have more energy because they get back more than they give to others.

Conversely, the speaker said that takers feel more depressed as they keep score and try to squeeze out an advantage to every deal. Takers waste opportunities to connect with others as they try to get everything they can in every interaction, trying to be the "winner" but losing in the end. Danny Thomas put it well when he said, "There are two types of people in this world: givers and takers. Takers always eat better, but givers always sleep better."

Emotional/Gratitude Bank Account

In another life, before I became a teacher, I worked in the business world. In one new employee training session, they went over the old business plan and a new business ideal. In the past, they said businesses went for the kill, trying to get every penny out of the customer in every deal, sometimes without regard for ethics. The new ideal is to create win/win situations, where we give the customer something in exchange for their long-term business, as well as establishing positive word of mouth.

At this training, they went on to talk about "emotional" back accounts. This was eye opening for me, to think that when we deal with people, we need to make deposits into their emotional bank accounts before we can make a withdrawal. For example, if we ask someone for a favor, they are more likely to do it if we have cultivated a relationship and have done something for them.

Like a bank account, we can't let our accounts get negative. I agree with that, but would go on to say the most successful people are the ones who realize they have enough to spread around and make deposits without keeping track. These are the true givers in life.

After teaching with gratitude for ten years, I would propose that we also have a "Gratitude Account" where the numbers matter. The more we practice gratitude and make it an action in our lives, the more happiness, connections, and joy we exude. In the classroom, on days when I am not so grateful, students will make deposits in my account and help me feel more grateful. I also try to fill up their accounts throughout the school year so they can make a withdrawal any time they need a little extra gratitude.

LAST CHALLENGE

Here is a final challenge: try to find a new way to give our time, talent, and treasure to our family, friends, colleagues, strangers, and the world. In our classrooms and lives, we can make deposits in other's gratitude accounts by finding something to be grateful for about someone and then expressing it. The challenge is to find a new person each day: a student, colleague, parent, or administrator, and make a deposit in their "gratitude" bank account. Then, watch as your "gratitude" account grows exponentially, affecting everyone in the world.

VITAMIN G AND GENERATION G

Some have referred to gratitude as "Vitamin G" because it is so powerful in our lives, the lives of our students, and their families. We all should keep taking our "Vitamin G" daily and giving it to everyone we know. There is a growing and limitless supply we tap into as we practice a conscious gratitude in our schools and make it part of our lives.

In their book *Making Grateful Kids*, Dr. Froh and Dr. Bono wrote about "Generation G." This is an encouraging idea, as we implement these ideas and actions of gratitude into our student's and children's lives, we are reshaping our youth into an entire generation that will form the world with gratitude.

STEPPING STONES TO GRATITUDE

1. The school year can be long and exhausting, but we experience priceless rewards as we practice gratitude with our students.
2. Writing gratitude letters in the classroom is one activity to helps promote a positive culture.
3. Make the effort to listen to our students, especially those that are challenges, changing the dynamics of the relationship with gratitude.
4. Make the conscious choice to be a "giver" and watch things improve in our classrooms and lives.

LET'S TALK ABOUT IT

1. Why is it hard to stay energized throughout the school year?
2. What are some approaches we can take to help rejuvenate as the school year progresses?
3. What are some tools we can use to help us survive and thrive as educators throughout our careers?

References

CHAPTER 1

1. Martin E. P. Seligman, *Flourish* (New York: Free Press, 2011), 30–31.

2. Rick Hanson, *Hardwiring Happiness, The New Brain Science of Contentment, Calm and Confidence* (New York: Harmony Books, 2013), 12–37.

3. Robert Emmons and Michael McCullough, "Counting Blessings versus Burdens: An Experimental Investigation of Gratitude and Subjective Well-Being in Daily Life," *Journal of Personality and Social Psychology* 84(2003): 377–89.

4. Rollin McCraty, et al., "The Impact of a New Emotional Self-Management Program on Stress, Emotions, and Heart Rate Variability, DHEA and Cortisol," *Integrative Physiology and Behavioral Science* (1998): 151–70.

5. Nancy Digdon and Amy Koble, "Effects of Constructive Worry, Imagery Distraction, and Gratitude Interventions on Sleep Quality: A Pilot Study," *Applied Psychology Health and Well Being* (2011): 193–206. Accessed March 23, 2015. DOI: 10.1111/j.1758-0854.2011.01049.

6. Nina Grant, Jane Wardle, and Andrew Steptoe. "The Relationship between Life Satisfaction and Health Behavior: A Cross-cultural Analysis of Young Adults," *International Journal of Behavioral Medicine* (2009): 259–68.

7. S. C. Segerstrom, "Optimism, Goal Conflict, and Stress-related Immune Changes," *Journal of Behavioral Medicine* (2001): 441–64.

8. Michael E. McCullough, Robert A. Emmons, and Jo-Ann Tsang, "The Grateful Disposition: A Conceptual and Empirical Topography," *Journal of Personality and Social Psychology* (2002): 112–27. Accessed March 29, 2015. DOI: 10.1037//0022-3514.82.1.112.

9. Alex M. Wood, Jeffrey J. Froh, and Adam W. A. Geraghty. "Gratitude and Well-being: A Review and Theoretical Integration," *Clinical Psychology Review* (2010): 890–905.

10. C. N. Dewall, N. H. Lambert, R. S. Pond, T. B. Kasdhan, and F. D. Fincham. "A Grateful Heart is a Nonviolent Heart: Cross-Sectional, Experience Sampling,

Longitudinal, and Experimental Evidence," *Social Psychology and Personality Science* (2012): 232–40.

11. Patrick L. Hill, Mathias Allemand, and Brent W. Roberts. "Examining the Pathways between Gratitude and Self-Rated Physical Health across Adulthood," *Personality and Individual Differences* (2013): 92–96.

12. Deepak Chopra, "Gratitude Journaling May Enhance Health in Cardiac Patients," *Huffington Post*. Accessed March 31, 2015. DOI: www.huffingtonpost.com/deepak-chopra/gratitude-journaling-may-_b_6976926.html.

13. Paul Mills, et al., "Effects of Gratitude Journaling on Heart Rate Variability and Inflammatory Biomarkers in Asymptomatic Heart Failure Patients." (Paper presented April, 2015 at the University of California, San Diego Institute for Public Health's Annual Public Health Research Day).

CHAPTER 2

1. A Complaint Free World Web Site. Accessed December 2, 2014. DOI: www.acomplaintfreeworld.org.

CHAPTER 3

1. Marsha L. Richins and Scott Dawson, "A Consumer Values Orientation for Materialism and its Measurement: Scale Development and Validation," *Journal of Consumer Research* 19(1992): 303–16. Accessed January 3, 2015. DOI: 10.1086/209304.

2. Jo-Ann Tsang, Thomas P. Carpenter, James A. Roberts, Michael B. Frisch, and Robert D. Carlisle, "Why are Materialists Less Happy? The Role of Gratitude and Need Satisfaction in the Relationship between Materialism and Life Satisfaction," *Personality and Individual Differences* 64 (2014): 62–66.

3. Jason Marsh and Dacher Keltner, "How Gratitude Beats Materialism," *Greater Good: The Science of a Meaningful Life*. Accessed January 8, 2015. http://greatergood.berkeley.edu/article/item/materialism_gratitude_happiness.

4. Tim Kasser and Richard M. Ryan, "A Dark Side of the American Dream: Correlates of Financial Success as a Central Life Aspiration," *Journal of Personality and Social Psychology* 65(1993): 410–22. Accessed February 9, 2015. DOI: org/10.1037/0022-3514.65.2.410.

5. Nathaniel M. Lambert, Frank D. Fincham, Tyler F. Stillman, and Lukas R. Dean, "More Gratitude, Less Materialism: The Mediating Role of Life Satisfaction," *The Journal of Positive Psychology* 4(2009): 32–42.

6. Christine Carter, Christine Carter's Blog, "11 Ways to Raise a Child who is Entitled and Rude." Accessed June 8, 2015. DOI: https://www.christinecarter.com/community/blog/2015/06/11-ways-to-raise-a-child-who-is-entitled-and-rude/.

CHAPTER 4

1. Robert Emmons, "Five Myths about Gratitude," *Greater Good: The Science of a Meaningful Life*. Accessed November 21, 2013. DOI: http://greatergood.berkeley.edu/article/item/five_myths_about_gratitude.

2. Philip C. Watkins, Lilia Cruz, Heather Holben, and Russell L. Kolts, "Taking Care if Business, Grateful Processing of Unpleasant Memories," *Journal of Positive Psychology 4(2008):* 87–99.

3. Sonja Lyubomerski, *The How of Happiness* (New York: Penguin Press, 2009), 21–23, 44, 53–58, 76–89.

CHAPTER 5

1. Brother David Steindl-Rast, *On Being Podcast: The Anatomy of Gratefulness*, January 21, 2016. Accessed January 22, 2016. DOI: http://www.onbeing.org/program/david-steindl-rast-anatomy-of-gratitude/8361.

2. Araceli Frias, Philip C. Watkins, Amy C. Webber, and Jeffrey J. Froh, "Death and Gratitude: Death Reflection Enhances Gratitude," *The Journal of Positive Psychology* 6(2011): 154–62.

3. Timothy Van Duivendyck, *The Unwanted Gift of Grief* (New York: Routledge, 2006), 12–19.

4. Scott Poland and Donna Poland, "Dealing with Death at School," *National Association of School Psychologist Online*. Accessed September 26, 2015. DOI: www.nasponline.org/resources/principals/Dealing%20with%20Death%20at%20School%20April%2004.pdf.

5. David Schonfeld, *The Grieving Student: A Teacher's Guide* (Maryland: Brooks Publishing, 2010), 22–30, 76–90.

CHAPTER 6

1. James A. Roberts, Luc Honore, Petnji Yaya, and Chris Manolis , "The Invisible Addiction: Cell-phone Activities and Addiction Among Male and Female College Students," *Journal of Behavioral Addiction* (2014): 254–65.

2. W. H. Dietz, Jr. and S. L. Gortmaker, "Do We Fatten our Children at the Television Set? Obesity and Television Viewing in Children and Adolescents," *Pediatrics* (1987): 807–12.

3. Tim Elmore, "Nomophobia, A Rising Trend in Students." Accessed May 15, 2015. DOI: https://www.psychologytoday.com/blog/artificial-maturity/201409/nomophobia-rising-trend-in-students.

4. Center on Media and Child Health Website. Accessed May 10, 2015. DOI: http://cmch.tv/parents.

CHAPTER 7

1. Jeffrey J. Froh, William J. Sefick, and Robert A. Emmons, "Counting Blessings in Early Adolescents: An Experimental Study of Gratitude and Subjective Well-Being," *Journal of School Psychology* 46(2008): 213–33.

2. Robert Emmons, "How Gratitude can get you through Hard Times," *Greater Good: The Science of a Meaningful Life* (2013). Accessed April 17, 2015. DOI: http://greatergood.berkeley.edu/article/item/how_gratitude_can_help_you_through_hard_times.

3. Robert A. Emmons and Michael E. McCullough, "Counting Blessings Versus Burdens: An Experimental Investigation of Gratitude and Subjective Well-Being in Daily Life," *Journal of Personality and Social Psychology* 84(2003): 377–89.

CHAPTER 8

1. Kimberly A. Schonert-Reichl, et al., "Enhancing Cognitive and Social–Emotional Development through a Simple-to-Administer Mindfulness-Based School Program for Elementary School Children: A Randomized Controlled Trial," *Developmental Psychology* 51(2015): 52–66.

2. Lisa Flook, et al., "Mindfulness for Teachers: A Pilot Study to Assess Effects on Stress, Burnout, and Teaching Efficacy," *Mind, Brain, and Education*, September, 2013, 182–195. Accessed April 3, 2015. DOI: 10.1111/mbe.12026.

3. Vicki Zakrzewski, "Can Mindfulness Make Us Better Teachers?" *Greater Good: The Science of a Meaningful Life* (2013). Accessed February 16, 2015. DOI: http://greatergood.berkeley.edu/article/item/can_mindfulness_make_us_better_teachers.

4. Thich Nhat Hanh, *The Miracle of Mindfulness: An Introduction to the Practice of Meditation* (Boston: Beacon Press, 1999), 11–29, 70–85.

5. Matthew A. Killingsworth and Daniel T. Gilbert, "A Wandering Mind Is an Unhappy Mind," *Science* 330(2010): 932. Accessed April 2, 2015. *DOI:* 10.1126/science.1192439.

CHAPTER 9

1. Francis Jensen, *The Teenage Brain*, (New York: Harper, 2015), 12–27, 44–9.

2. Robert Emmons, "Pay it Forward," *Greater Good: The Science of a Meaningful Life* (2007). Accessed March 17, 2015. Accessed March 30, 21015. DOI: http://greatergood.berkeley.edu/article/item/pay_it_forward/.

3. L. N. Chaplin, A. Rindfleisch, D.R. John, and J. J. Froh, "Reducing Materialism in Adolescents." Submitted for publication, 2013.

4. Jeffrey Froh and Giacomo Bono, *Making Grateful Kids, The Science of Building Character*, (Pennsylvania: Templeton Press, 2014) 146–147.

5. Giacomo Bono, "Searching for the Developmental Role of Gratitude: A 4-year Longitudinal Analysis," American Psychological Association website (2012). Accessed March 27, 2015. DOI: http://www.apa.org/news/press/releases/2012/08/health-benefits.aspx.

6. Jeffrey J. Froh, William J. Sefick, and Robert A. Emmons, "Counting blessings in early adolescents: An experimental study of gratitude and subjective well-being," *Journal of School Psychology* 46 (2008): 213–233.

7. Jeffrey J. Froh, Robert A. Emmons, Noel A. Card, Giacomo Bono, and Jennifer A. Wilson, "Gratitude and the Reduced Costs of Materialism in Adolescents," *Journal of Happiness Studies*, 12 (2010). Accessed March 4, 2015. DOI: 10.1007/s10902-010-9195-9.

8. Christine Carter, *Raising Happiness*, (New York: Ballantine Books, 2010), 30–37.

CHAPTER 10

1. M. E. Seligman, T. A. Steen, N. Park, and C. Peterson, "Positive Psychology Progress: Empirical Validation of Interventions," *American Psychologist* 60(2005): 410.

2. Dr. Jeffrey Froh, Interview March 28, 2015.

CHAPTER 11

1. Robert Emmons, *Thanks, A 21-Day Program* (California: Jossey-Bass, 2013), 51–72.

2. Vicki Zakrzewski, "Gratitude Activities for Classroom," *Greater Good: The Science of a Meaningful Life* (2013). Accessed November 22, 2014. DOI: http://greatergood.berkeley.edu/article/item/gratitude_activities_for_the_classroom.

3. Parker Palmer interview: *On Being Podcast*, January 5, 2015. Accessed June 9, 2015. DOI: http://www.onbeing.org/program/transcript/7194.

4. James Baraz and and Shoshana Alexander, "The Helper's High," *Greater Good: The Science of a Meaningful Life* (2010). Accessed May 4, 2015. DOI: http://greatergood.berkeley.edu/article/item/the_helpers_high.

5. Christine Carter, *Raising Happiness,* (New York: Ballantine Books, 2010), 57–59.

CHAPTER 12

1. Jeffrey Froh and Giacomo Bono, *Making Grateful Kids, The Science of Building Character* (Pennsylvania: Templeton Press, 2014), 127–30.

Gratitude Resources

Books, Organizations, and Websites

BOOKS

Making Grateful Kids by Dr. Jeffrey Froh and Dr. Giacomo Bono
This is a wonderful book for parents, teachers, or anyone who has contact with children. Dr. Froh and Dr. Bono balance research with insights and practical activities.
Thanks, a 21-Day Program by Dr. Robert Emmons
This book helps explore gratitude and gives a twenty-one-day plan that is helpful to integrating gratitude into our lives. Dr. Emmons gives interesting stories and strong foundation of research.
Gratitude, the Heart of Prayer by Brother David Steindl-Rast
Brother Steindl-Rast helped introduce me to gratitude with this book. Many spiritual insights abound throughout the pages.

SOCIAL-EMOTIONAL LEARNING
AND MINDFULNESS ORGANIZATIONS

Note: Many of these organizations utilize gratitude in their education programs.
CASEL (Collaboration for Academic, Social and Emotional Learning): http://www
.casel.org/
Center for Investigating Healthy Minds: http://www.investigatinghealthyminds.org/
Collaborative Classroom: https://www.collaborativeclassroom.org/
Committee for Children: http://www.cfchildren.org/
HopeLab: http://www.hopelab.org/
Inner Resilience: http://innerresilience-tidescenter.org/
Leading Together: http://www.couragerenewal.org/leadingtogether/
MindUp-The Hawn Foundation: http://thehawnfoundation.org/mindup/
Mindful Schools: http://www.mindfulschools.org/training/mindfulness-fundamentals/

The David Lynch Foundation: https://www.davidlynchfoundation.org/schools.html
New Teacher Center: http://newteachercenter.org/
Open Circle: http://www.open-circle.org/
University of California, Los Angeles, Mindful Awareness Research Center: http://marc.ucla.edu/body.cfm?id=22

WEBSITES

The Center on Media and Child Health: http://cmch.tv/parents
Dealing with Death at School: www.naspcenter.org/principals/nassp_death.html
Dr. Emmon's Website: http://emmons.faculty.ucdavis.edu/links/
Greater Good Science Center: http://www.greatergood.berkeley.edu/
Gratitude Activities: http://greatergood.berkeley.edu/article/item/gratitude_activities_for_the_classroom
Gratitude Curriculum: http://people.hofstra.edu/jeffrey_j_froh/Gratitude%20Lesson%20Plans_Final_10.26.10.pdf
Greater Good Gratitude Quiz: http://greatergood.berkeley.edu/quizzes/take_quiz/6
Online Gratitude Activities: http://ggia.berkeley.edu/#filters=gratitude
VIA Character Strength's Inventory: http://www.viacharacter.org/www/

Index

Acknowledgments

First of all, I would like to thank my sister, Diane, for helping edit this book even though she was in Saudi Arabia and busy with other endeavors. Another huge gratitude goes out to my brothers and sisters: Carolyn, Danny, Nancy, Larry, Mary, and Steve (you are still with us) for their love and gratitude that grows throughout the years. This book would not have been possible without the love, support, and example of gratitude that my parents gave me. Thank you, Mom and Dad!

In addition, I would like to acknowledge the tremendous and indispensable help of Bruce McPherson, who embodies gratitude in every aspect of his life and is a sagacious mentor. I am very thankful for Dr. Jeff Froh who helped me immensely with this book, every step of the way, including writing the foreword. Jeff has also been a good friend and mentor. Another grateful friend and mentor is Dr. Giacomo Bono, whose encouragement and inclusion in the Gratitude Conference helped enormously with this book.

Also, a huge thank you goes to my publisher and editor Sarah Jubar, who discovered my article on Edutopia, encouraged me to submit a book proposal, and did a fantastic job editing this book. I also appreciate Laura Gallinari, who encouraged me to start the blog and taught me so many spiritual lessons in and out of the classroom. In addition, I would like to thank Anna Entz and Krissy Fields who were fantastic partner-teachers and applied gratitude in new and fun ways.

Thank you to Giacomu Bono, Greg Doss, Robert Emmons, Jeffrey Froh, Erik Herndon, Philip Watkins, and Vicki Zakrewski for their articulate and insightful endorsements. I would also like to acknowledge Dr. David Rhodes, who encouraged me to write down everything that happened in the classroom because I might use it someday. It all went into this book. Finally, I would like to give my thanks to Elaine Stannard, my former high school counselor, who came back into my life to help edit my book proposal.

About the Author

Owen M. Griffith is a fourth-grade teacher and guitar instructor, residing with his wife and son in North Georgia. He earned a master's degree in Educational Leadership. Owen's work has appeared on Huffington Post and Edutopia. Check out his blog at www.spirituallyteaching.blogspot.com, online at www .facebook.com/griffithgratitude, or email him at griffitho@hotmail.com. Owen is available for speaking engagements, educational consulting, and professional developments.